Biggest Bugs Life-Size

George Beccaloni

A FIREFLY BOOK

Published by Firefly Books Ltd. 2010

Second Printing, 2014

Publisher Cataloging-in-Publication Data (U.S.)

Beccaloni, George.
 Biggest bugs life-size / George Beccaloni.
[84] p. : col. photos., maps ; cm.
Includes bibliographic references and index.
Summary: Life-size photographs of the world's largest and most spectacular bugs, with the essential facts including: where they live, what they eat, and who discovered them.
ISBN-13: 978-1-55407-699-4 (pbk.)
1. Insects – Size. 2. Insects. I. Title.
595.7 dc22   QL467.2B433 2010

Library and Archives Canada Cataloguing in Publication

Beccaloni, George
 Biggest bugs life-size / George Beccaloni.
Includes bibliographical references and index.
ISBN 978-1-55407-699-4
 1. Insects--Size. 2. Insects--Size--Pictorial works. I. Title.
QL463.B43 2010   595.714'1   C2010-900133-8

Published in the United States by
Firefly Books (U.S.) Inc.
P.O. Box 1338, Ellicott Station
Buffalo, New York 14205

Published in Canada by
Firefly Books Ltd.
50 Staples Avenue, Unit 1
Richmond Hill, Ontario L4B 0A7

Printed in China at C&C Offset Printing Co

I dedicate this book to my wonderful wife Jan, who is also fascinated by bugs – especially ones with eight legs.

Cover design Ruth Hope
Designed by Mercer Design, London
Cartographer Lisa Wilson
Reproduction by Saxon Digital Services
Printed by C&C Offset

Contents

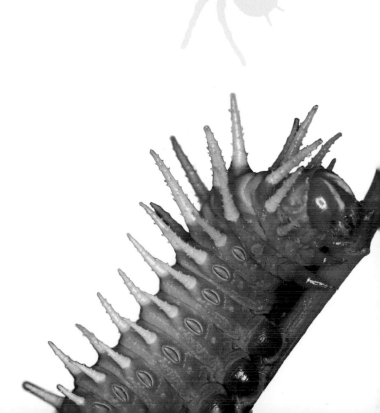

Introduction

According to entomologists (scientists who study insects) bugs are insects with mouthparts adapted for sucking up liquids. They belong to a large group of species called the Hemiptera, and examples are bed bugs, aphids and cicadas. However, in popular terminology, bug is used to refer to any insect, and in this book its definition also covers all non-marine arthropods (animals with external skeletons and jointed legs) excluding crustaceans such as crabs. Other popular terms for these creatures are creepy crawlers (in North America), creepy crawlies (in the UK), and minibeasts. The bugs featured are the largest representatives of all the major groups, called orders by scientists, of insects, arachnids (spiders and their relatives) and myriapods (centipedes and millipedes) that contain at least one species with an adult body length of 1¾ in (50 mm) or more.

What is meant by biggest?

The term biggest means different things to different people when referring to the sizes of bugs and other creatures. Some might argue that the biggest species is the one with the greatest body length, others that it is the one with the greatest wingspan, and yet others might say that it is the heaviest species. I think that the best measure of size is the body weight of the living animal, but to satisfy as many people as possible I

▼ The heaviest stick insect is an adult female jungle nymph from Southeast Asia. Here it is shown life-size.

have decided to include not only the heaviest species of a group (where this information is known), but also the species that has either the largest body length or greatest wingspan, whichever is the larger of the two. In many cases this is the heaviest species anyway. There are, however, three exceptions to this rule.

For beetles, I focus on the species with the greatest body lengths, despite the fact that the wingspans of these and some other beetles are considerably greater than the body lengths of the longest species. This is because body length is the traditional measure of size for these insects, and also because the wingspans of most beetles are unknown – the wings of beetles are folded up under their wing cases and are therefore difficult to examine. The second exception is moths, where, in addition to the heaviest species and species with the greatest wingspan, I also include the species with the largest wing area. The final exception is spiders, where as well as the heaviest species, I feature the species with the largest leg-span rather than greatest body length.

Body length is measured in a straight line from the tip of the mandibles (jaws), or the longest forward-projecting horn, to the end of the abdomen, minus any unnatural gap between the thorax and the abdomen. Beetles are measured to the end of their wing cases or abdomen, whichever is longer. Other structures such as the antennae and the egg-laying tube or ovipositor, which females of some bugs have, are excluded. Wingspan is calculated as twice the distance from the tip of the forewing, or hindwing in the case of beetles, to the base of the wing in a straight line, plus the distance between the bases of the wings. The advantage of this is that the wings can be arranged in any position and you still get the same wingspan. Please note that the imperial measurements used in this book are approximate and for accuracy the metric measurements should be used.

▼ How the bugs in this book are measured. This is a male (life-size) of the world's biggest wasp, the giant tarantula-hawk wasp. The female is about double the size.

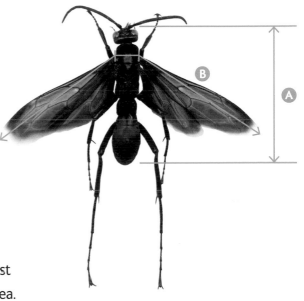

Ⓐ Body length   Ⓑ Wingspan

There are many problems with measuring the length of bugs, including stretching of specimens (deliberately or not), shrinkage of the body after death (a common problem with soft-bodied species), and deciding what dimensions to measure in the first place. There are also problems with using weight as a measure of size. Weights of living specimens are usually unknown, especially those of the largest individuals of a particular species. Weight also varies according to factors such as how well fed individuals are at the time they were weighed and, in the case of pregnant females, how many eggs they are carrying and how large these are. One problem with weighing dead specimens is that they may or may not contain dried body contents – these will have rotted away to a greater or lesser extent. Also, because the body contents have dried up, most of the weight is made up of the exoskeleton (the often rigid, outer covering of a bug's body). This means there could be awkward situations where a larger bug, in terms of body volume, weighs less when dead than a smaller dead bug with a much thicker and therefore heavier exoskeleton – even though the larger bug might have weighed more when alive!

A gigantic grub

In advanced insects such as butterflies, beetles and flies, which have life-cycles with complete metamorphosis (they have larval, pupal and adult stages, rather than just nymphs like more primitive insects), the larvae are always considerably heavier than the adults. This is because a lot of weight is lost during the transformation from larva to adult during the pupal stage. Although many books and articles say that the world's heaviest insect is an adult beetle (e.g. an African Goliath beetle) or the wetapunga from New Zealand, this book reveals that it is actually the fully grown larva of the South American Actaeon beetle, which weighs as much as 7.6 English sparrows. When discussing the weights of insects, people usually forget about the larvae!

▼ The world's heaviest bug. A fully grown male larva of the South American Actaeon beetle bred in Japan in 2009 by Mr Takayuki Suzuki. It weighs an incredible 8 oz (228 g).

Fantastically large fossils

The largest living bugs are dwarfed by giant fossil species. The fossil millipede-like *Arthropleura* from the Late Carboniferous about 300 million years ago, is the largest terrestrial arthropod known to have ever existed. It could grow to an amazing 8½ ft (2.6 m) long and is thought to have been a herbivore.

The largest insect of all time is the predatory giant dragonfly-like *Meganeuropsis permiana*, which lived during the Permian about 280 million years ago. It had a wingspan of just over 27½ in (700 mm) and an estimated body length of around 17 in (430 mm). Perhaps surprisingly, the largest known representatives of many groups of bugs, such as cockroaches and spiders, are not fossil species as you might expect, but species which are still alive today.

▲ Scene from a Carboniferous coal swamp. *Arthropleura* crawls over a fallen log, whilst the giant dragonfly-like *Meganeura* searches for its prey. *Meganeura* had a wingspan of about 23½ in (600 mm).

Amazonian Giant Centipede

WORLD'S BIGGEST CENTIPEDE

Maximum body length (adult, sex unknown):
13¾ in (350 mm)

Scientific name: *Scolopendra gigantea*

Distribution: Aruba, Curaçao, Margarita Island, Trinidad, northern Venezuela, Colombia and Suriname

▲ The Amazonian giant centipede lives in seasonally dry habitats ranging from thorn scrub to dry tropical forest. As it is a nocturnal creature it spends much of the daytime in moist underground burrows.

ronically, the Amazonian giant centipede has only once been recorded from the Amazon region. Most of the known specimens are from northern South America and neighboring islands in the southern Caribbean. This formidable creature feeds voraciously on a wide range of prey, including invertebrates such as cockroaches, crickets, beetles and tarantulas. It also eats small vertebrates such as frogs, lizards, mice and birds.

▼ Male and female Amazonian giant centipedes are very similar in appearance and adults are usually about 7⅞ in (200 mm) in length. This image is life-size.

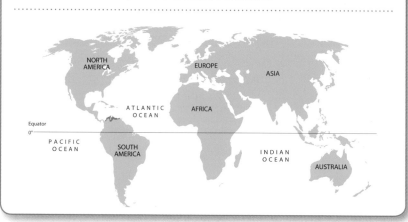

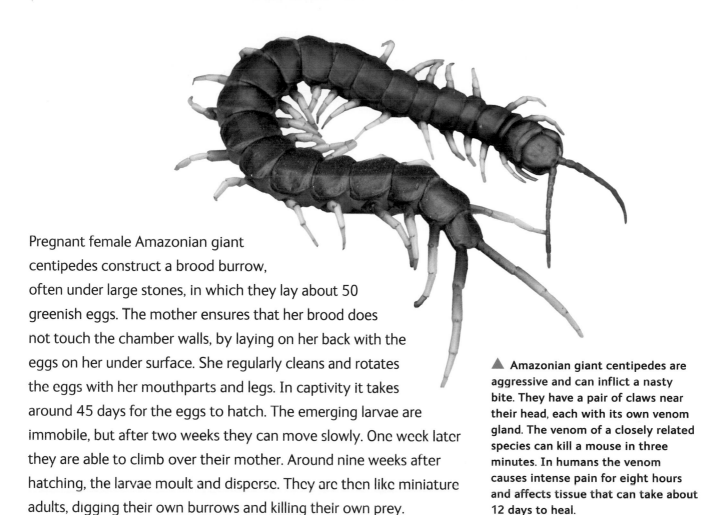

Pregnant female Amazonian giant centipedes construct a brood burrow, often under large stones, in which they lay about 50 greenish eggs. The mother ensures that her brood does not touch the chamber walls, by laying on her back with the eggs on her under surface. She regularly cleans and rotates the eggs with her mouthparts and legs. In captivity it takes around 45 days for the eggs to hatch. The emerging larvae are immobile, but after two weeks they can move slowly. One week later they are able to climb over their mother. Around nine weeks after hatching, the larvae moult and disperse. They are then like miniature adults, digging their own burrows and killing their own prey.

The longest known specimen is an old, dried individual in the Muséum National d'Histoire Naturelle, Paris, with a body length of 14½ in (370 mm). However, it has been slightly stretched and it is thought that when alive it would have been nearer to 13¾ in (350 mm). It is not known how much a specimen of this size would weigh, but an individual that was 9¼ in (240 mm) long weighed 1⅛ oz (33.35 g).

▲ Amazonian giant centipedes are aggressive and can inflict a nasty bite. They have a pair of claws near their head, each with its own venom gland. The venom of a closely related species can kill a mouse in three minutes. In humans the venom causes intense pain for eight hours and affects tissue that can take about 12 days to heal.

▲ Amazonian giant centipedes have been filmed in a limestone cave in Venezuela. They were hanging down from the ceiling and catching flying bats with their front eight pairs of legs!

Giant African Millipede

WORLD'S BIGGEST MILLIPEDE

Maximum body length (adult, sex unknown): 15⅛ in (387 mm)

Scientific name: *Archispirostreptus gigas*

Distribution: Somalia, Kenya, Tanzania, Zanzibar, Mozambique and northeast South Africa

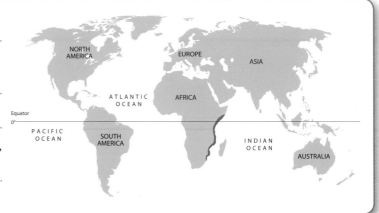

▲ The giant African millipede lives in dry forests and savannah woodlands in East and southern Africa at altitudes below about 3,281 ft (1,000 m).

Female giant African millipedes are nocturnal, and hide under rocks and dead wood during the day. At night they feed on dead and decaying plant matter, such as dead leaves, decaying wood and fallen fruit. They construct a brood chamber in moist soil into which they lay several hundred eggs. The eggs are coated with a protective layer of soil mixed with a secretion from the female's rectum. They hatch

▶ When threatened, giant African millipedes coil up into a tight spiral, protecting their more vulnerable "undercarriage" and their head. This image is life-size.

in 1–2 months and the young that emerge have no appendages. Even after moulting, the young still do not look much like adults, because they are white, have only a few body segments and only three pairs of legs. As they develop, they pass through several more moults. At each moult, they get a greater number of body segments and more pairs of legs, and become darker. The giant African millipede takes three to four years to reach maturity and has a life span of 10–12 years in captivity and approximately seven years in the wild.

Giant African millipedes coil up to defend themselves and emit a strong-smelling, foul-tasting fluid through a pair of tiny pores on the sides of each body segment. They only discharge the chemicals from those segments that are threatened. The defensive secretions of this millipede are relatively mild.

The longest known individual of this species was a captive specimen owned by Jim Klinger of Texas, U.S., which had a body length of 15⅛ in (387 mm) and a circumference of 2½ in (67 mm). This is the world's longest known bug.

▼ Adult giant African millipedes have up to 250 legs. They usually grow to between 5½–12½ in (140–320 mm) long with a diameter of ¼–¾ in (11–21 mm). This image is life-size.

Goliath Bird-Eating Spider

WORLD'S HEAVIEST SPIDER

Maximum weight (adult female):
6⅛ oz (175 g)

Scientific name: *Theraphosa blondi*

Distribution: Southern Venezuela, Guyana, Suriname, French Guiana and northeast Brazil

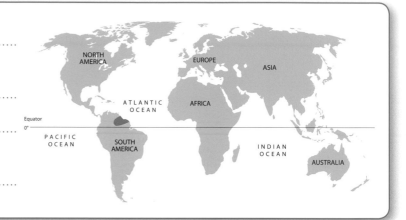

◀ **Despite its common name, the Goliath bird-eater is an opportunistic hunter and doesn't normally eat birds. Its usual prey are insects such as beetles and crickets, but it also eats small mammals, reptiles and frogs. As a rule of thumb, it generally tries to eat anything smaller than itself!**

The enormous Goliath bird-eating spider is most frequently found in mountain rainforests, where the humidity is always high and the soil and leaf litter are always damp. It lives in cavities under rocks, fallen logs or in abandoned rodent or lizard burrows. It is nocturnal and spends most of its time in its silk-lined burrow.

Female Goliath bird-eaters lay around 50–150 eggs in a huge silk egg sac 1⅛ in (30 mm) in diameter, which the mother carries around with her. The spiderlings emerge from it after about two months and have a legspan of about ½ in (19 mm). They may live in their mother's burrow until they have grown to one third of their full size.

Goliath bird-eaters take 2.5–3 years to reach maturity and can live up to 20 years. Males die soon after mating and have a lifespan of only 3–6 years. Like other tarantulas, adult Goliath bird-eaters continue to moult, enabling them to regenerate any limbs that have been damaged or lost.

Goliath bird-eaters make a hissing noise to warn off potential enemies by rubbing together the bristles on their first two pairs of legs and pedipalps, or front appendages. If they feel highly threatened they throw their first two pairs of legs back, open their fangs and hinge them upwards so that they are perfectly positioned to bite their attacker. They can also flick barb-tipped hairs from their abdomens at potential predators, using their hind legs. These hairs can severely irritate the skin, nose and eyes of mammals, including humans.

The heaviest recorded female was a 12-year-old captive specimen called Rosi, which in 2007 had a body length of 4½ in (119.4 mm) and weighed an amazing 6⅛ oz (175 g).

◀ As with most spiders, the female is heavier than the male. Males have a body length up to 3½ in (90 mm) and a legspan up to 11 in (280 mm), while females have a legspan up to 10½ in (267 mm) (measured from leg 1 to leg 4 on the same side) and weigh on average about 2¼ oz (65 g). This image is life-size.

◀ To catch its food, the Goliath bird-eater relies mainly on sensing vibrations through the surface it is standing on, because – like most spiders – it has very poor eyesight. When it detects potential prey, it dashes out of its burrow and pierces the victim with its ¾ in (20 mm) long fangs. This image is life-size.

Giant Huntsman Spider

SPIDER WITH GREATEST LEGSPAN

Maximum legspan (adult male):
11¾ in (300 mm)

Scientific name: *Heteropoda maxima*

Distribution: Laos (Khammouane province)

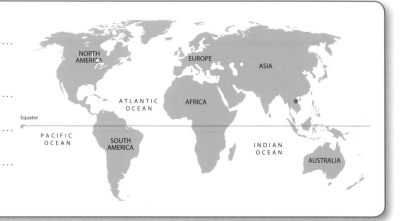

▶ The giant huntsman spider is only known from limestone caves in central Laos. It lives near the entrances and up to 98 ft (30 m) or more inside the caves. Although it is not obviously adapted to cave life (truly cave-adapted animals often have features such as pale bodies, and eyes that are small or absent), it has not been found in the forest around the caves.

Like Chan's megastick, the longest bug in the world (see p.42), this humongous spider was only given its scientific name quite recently. It was appropriately christened *maxima* (the largest) in 2001 from specimens collected by Mademoiselle Colani in 1930 and 1933, which had been preserved in the Muséum National d'Histoire Naturelle, Paris.

Giant huntsman spiders don't build webs but wait for insects and other small creatures to wander close enough to grab. They live on the smooth cave walls and can move very quickly when disturbed. There are reports that living spiders are being collected for sale to enthusiasts in Germany. Since species that live in caves usually occur in low numbers, because of the scarcity of food, collecting could easily damage the population. The largest known individual of this species is an adult male collected in 1933 in the collection of the Muséum National d'Histoire Naturelle, Paris. It has a legspan of 11¾ in (300 mm) (from the tip of the second leg on one side of the body to the tip of the corresponding leg on the other side). One pregnant female had a body length of about 1¾ in (50 mm) from its jaws to the tip of its abdomen, whereas males have a body length of about 1⅛ in (30 mm). It might surprise many people to learn that this species has a larger legspan than any tarantula! The largest legspan of 11 in (280 mm) was reliably recorded for a male Goliath bird eating spider (see p.12), a tarantula, collected in Venezuela in 1965.

▲ Females produce a flat, circular sac of white papery silk into which they lay their eggs. They carry this under their bodies until shortly before the eggs hatch. Then the mother attaches the sac to the cave wall and guards it until the spiderlings emerge.

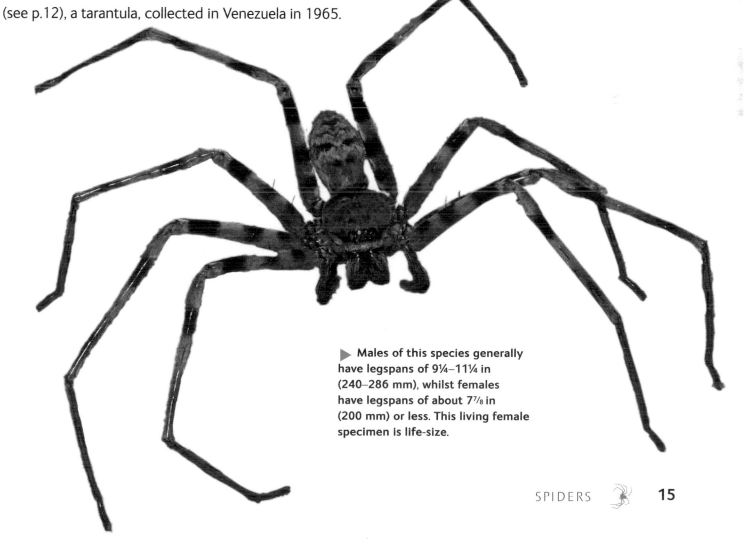

▶ Males of this species generally have legspans of 9¼–11¼ in (240–286 mm), whilst females have legspans of about 7⅞ in (200 mm) or less. This living female specimen is life-size.

Giant Vinegaroon

WORLD'S BIGGEST UROPYGID

Maximum weight (adult female): $3/7$ oz (12.4 g)

Scientific name: *Mastigoproctus giganteus*

Distribution: Southern Florida and southwest U.S. to southern Mexico

▲ The formidable-looking giant vinegaroon lives in dry habitats from desert and chaparral to pine forests, grassland and scrub in the south of North America. They are nocturnal and hide during the day in non-permanent burrows they dig themselves, in rodent burrows or rock crevices, or under rocks, logs or other objects.

When hunting, the giant vinegaroon moves slowly, exploring objects by "feeling" with its elongated front legs. When it comes across prey, it quickly seizes its victim, and crushes it using its heavily armored pedipalps, or front appendages. Uropygids spray a mixture of chemicals from their anal glands, to deter predators. One chemical in the mixture is acetic acid, which is the main component of vinegar – hence their common name of vinegaroon. To aim the spray, the uropygid directs its anus towards the attacker; the spray can be directed very accurately. Invertebrate predators of uropygids, such as solifugids, are particularly sensitive to acetic acid, showing signs of distress such as jaw-rubbing behavior. With humans and vertebrate predators such as birds, reptiles and mice, the defensive chemical affects the eyes and respiratory tract.

◀ Giant vinegaroons feed on a wide variety of invertebrates, such as crickets, beetles, cockroaches and spiders. There have also been reports of them feeding on small vertebrates like frogs and toads. This image is life-size.

◀ A female giant vinegaroon lays 7 35 eggs in a transparent sac which she carries under her body.

After hatching from their eggs, young giant vinagaroons climb on their mother's back and remain there for several weeks. Neither the young nor their mother feed during this time and after the young have moulted they disperse, leaving behind their starved mother who often dies soon afterwards. It takes giant vinegaroons around three to four years to reach adulthood and they can live for up to seven years.

Male and female giant vinegaroons look very similar. One of the subtle differences between them lies in their pedipalps – in females, they are short and stout, but in males they are longer and are used when males fight each other. The heaviest specimen known was an adult female which weighed ³/₇ oz (12.4 g). The heaviest adult male recorded weighed ¼ oz (10.2 g) and the longest specimen known (a female) had a body length of 3¹/₈ in (82 mm) (not including the tail).

▼ The body length of an adult giant vinegaroons ranges from 1¾ to 2¼ in (45 to 60 mm) and large individuals weigh around ¼ oz (7.7 g). Unlike a scorpion tail, the giant vinegaroon's tail is not part of its abdomen. This image is life-size.

Giant Solifugids

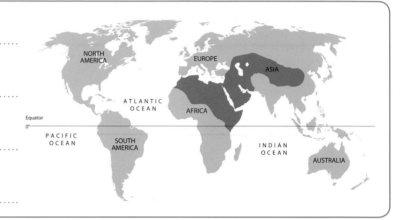

WORLD'S BIGGEST SOLIFUGIDS

Maximum weight (adult, sex unknown):
1¾ oz (56 g)

Scientific name: *Galeodes arabs, caspius* and *granti*

Distribution: Northern and East Africa, the Middle East, Central Asia and the Far East

▲ **These formidable creatures live in arid habitats from northern Africa, the Middle East and Central Asia to China. Being strictly nocturnal, they rest in their burrows during the day.**

The accolade of world's biggest solifugid probably belongs to not one, but to three closely related species: the Egyptian giant solifugid (*Galeodes arabs*), the Central Asian giant solifugid (*G. caspius*) and the banded giant solifugid (*G. granti*). Egyptian and banded solifugids live in horizontal convoluted burrows which are 7⅞ in (200 mm) below the surface. These often extend for several meters. Egyptian solifugid burrows are often found at the bases of plants. In damp weather, these solifugids might sit at the burrow entrance, but during hot weather, they plug the entrance with leaves and retreat to the innermost depths. The Central Asian solifugid constructs its burrows in sandy soils on southeast-facing slopes, to catch more sun. Solifugids often dig their own burrows by scooping up soil with their massive jaws, but they may also take unoccupied burrows and enlarge them.

Juvenile Central Asian solifugids use a "sit-and-wait strategy" in bushes, and hang from branches with their pedipalps, or front appendages, outstretched to catch flying prey. Adults forage actively on the ground, covering large distances. When a solifugid locates prey, it rapidly darts forward and captures it using its pedipalpal suckers and/or its jaws. It then macerates its victim, by moving it backwards and forwards through its jaws. As they run, solifugids keep their pedipalps extended in front of their body to locate prey. Solifugids can run extremely fast (up to 19½ in or 500 mm per second) in short frenetic bursts, and are among the fastest of all bugs. One of their common names is "wind spider," because they run like the wind!

Female Central Asian solifugids produce around 100 whitish, spherical eggs in a clutch whereas the banded solifugid produces only about 30 eggs. Central Asian solifugid larvae hatch after about 20 days. After hatching the young are not able to move until after they have moulted 20 days later. During the course of several more moults, they gradually become able to fend for themselves. Female giant solifugids protect their offspring within their brood burrow.

▲ The greatest weight recorded for a giant solifugid is 56 g (2 oz). The greatest legspan is 4½ in (120 mm). Their body length gets up to 2¾ in (70 mm). This specimen is shown life-size.

▼ Solifugids are some of the most important predators in arid environments. They normally prey on insects and arachnids, but they may feed on anything they can overpower, such as spiders, scorpions, small lizards and rodents.

◄ Solifugids are rather short-lived. They usually live for just one year, though captive individuals have survived for up to two years. Males die shortly after mating. Male giant solifugids are smaller and lighter than females, but have longer legs.

Emperor Scorpion

WORLD'S BIGGEST SCORPION

Maximum weight (adult, sex unknown): 2+ oz (60+ g)

Scientific name: *Pandinus imperator*

Distribution: From Guinea and Sierra Leone, through Liberia, Côte d'Ivoire, Ghana, Togo and Benin, into eastern Nigeria

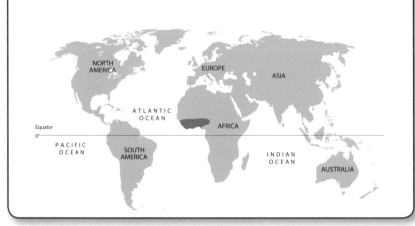

▼ Female emperor scorpions tend to be larger and more robust than males, but males tend to have a longer tail. The bulb at the end of the tail, called the telson, ends in a long sharp sting, which is used to inject venom. This image is life-size.

The handsome emperor scorpion is found in tropical rainforest bordering rivers and moist savannah in West Africa. This species lives in burrows 11¾ in (300 mm) long, in termite mounds, or beneath logs, rocks or tree roots. It uses its spade-like claws on its pedipalps, or front appendages, to excavate these burrows, or it may take over abandoned ones. It lives communally – there can be up to 20 related and unrelated individuals of mixed ages crowded into one burrow. The emperor scorpion is active at night and also during the day, which is very unusual for scorpions. After rain, individuals may be seen on the surface in considerable numbers.

Emperor scorpions feed on a wide range of invertebrates, especially millipedes and beetles, and scavenge small dead animals too. They are usually ambush predators, waiting motionless in the mouth of their burrow until passing prey comes within range. When it does, they rush out, grab it, and then retreat into the burrow to eat it. The hairs on the pedipalps are so sensitive that the emperor scorpion can detect and capture flying insects, as well as very quickly discriminating between suitable prey such as moths, potentially harmful creatures such as bees, and their own offspring.

Although large and formidable-looking, adult emperor scorpions rarely sting. They use their very large claws to crush their prey, as opposed to scorpions with slim claws, which usually sting their prey. In contrast, young emperors sting their prey – maybe because their claws are not as strong as those of adults. The venom of the emperor scorpion is painful but not dangerous to a healthy human.

Young emperor scorpions may live in the mother's burrow for two years or more. They reach sexual maturity at between 4–7 years old, and have a lifespan of about eight years.

The usual length of this species is 5⅛–7¹⁄₁₆ in (130–180 mm), with the forest form being considerably larger than the savannah form. This species is both the heaviest and longest of all the world's approximate 1,500 scorpion species. Individuals can weigh more than 2 oz (60 g) and a male from Sierra Leone caught in 1977 measured a record 9 in (229 mm) in length. Another male from Ghana caught in 1931 had a body length of 8¾ in (228 mm). The average weight of females without eggs is around 1 oz (30 g).

▼ All scorpions give birth to well-developed young. The emperor scorpion has a small brood size of 30–35. As the babies emerge, they are helped by their mother on to her back. She carries them around until after their first moult to protect them from predators.

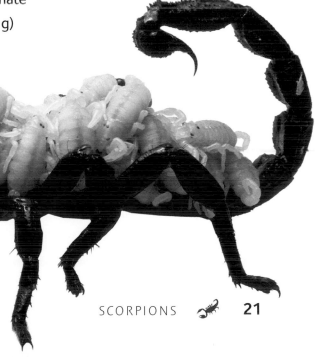

Giant Hawker Dragonfly

WORLD'S HEAVIEST ODONATE

Maximum weight (adult female): unknown

Scientific name: *Tetracanthagyna plagiata*

Distribution: Malay Peninsula, Singapore, Sumatra, Borneo

▲ The nymphs of the giant hawker live in streams in lowland rainforest, like this one in Singapore.

The giant hawker dragonfly lives in mature and regenerating lowland rainforest. Although it is probably not uncommon, it is rarely seen as it is mainly active at night and usually flies high in the forest canopy. It is sometimes attracted to artificial light at night and that is when people notice it.

Females have been seen laying eggs in rotting logs and branches above forest streams during the day and after hatching the nymphs crawl or fall into the water. Like the adults, the nymphs of all Odonata are carnivorous and those of the giant hawker probably eat invertebrates, tadpoles and fish. They catch their prey using an

unusual structure called the "mask" – an elongated lower lip which is hinged and can be extended at lightning speed to grab prey using two hooks at its end. The prey is then pulled towards the jaws and eaten.

Dragonfly nymphs breathe underwater through their anus, which is an enlarged cavity containing special folds to increase the surface area for gas exchange. They "inhale" by pumping water into the chamber, and "exhale" by squirting water out. A side benefit of this is jet propulsion. When a nymph is threatened by a predator or wants to move fast, it pulls its legs against its body and rapidly squirts the water out of its anal chamber, propelling it quickly forward.

Although no living specimens of the giant hawker dragonfly have been weighed, it is thought to be the heaviest of all Odonata because it is the bulkiest species. The largest known specimen is a female from Borneo in the collection of the Natural History Museum, London. It has a wingspan of 6¾ in (172 mm).

▲ Male giant hawker dragonflies are smaller than females and they, and some females like this one, lack the dark bands near the tips of the wings. Dragonflies hold their wings at right angles to their bodies when resting, unlike damselflies.

▶ The giant hawker has the largest wingspan of any dragonfly. This female specimen from Sumatra, has a wingspan of 6¼ in (160 mm), and is shown life-size.

Giant Helicopter Damselfly

ODONATE WITH GREATEST WINGSPAN

Maximum wingspan (adult male): 7¼ in (190 mm)

Scientific Name: *Megaloprepus caerulatus*

Distribution: Central America and northern and western South America

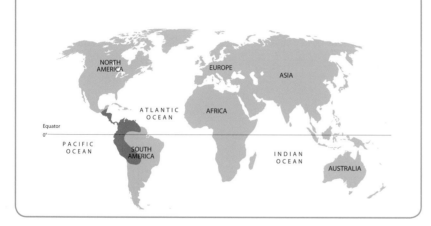

▲ During mating the male grasps the female behind her head and she picks up sperm from his second abdominal segment. All Odonata mate in this "wheel" position.

◄ Damselflies rest with their wings held together over their bodies, unlike dragonflies.

The giant helicopter damselfly is found in mature wet and seasonally dry forests from southern Mexico to Bolivia and eastward to Venezuela and Guyana. Adults can live for up to eight months and they spend a lot of their time flying slowly in gaps of light in the forest, hunting for the orb-weaving spiders that they feed on. When they spot a spider, they flutter a few feet away from it before darting forward and snatching it out of its web.

◀ A giant helicopter damselfly in flight, searching for the orb-weaving spiders that it feeds on.

▼ This adult male (shown life-size) from Costa Rica is in the Natural History Museum, London, and is the largest specimen known. It has a wingspan of 7¼ in (190 mm) and a body length of 4¾ in (121 mm). Unusually for Odonata, the females are smaller than the males.

Male giant helicopter damselflies, which are larger than the females, set up territories around water-filled holes and depressions in the trunks of fallen or living trees. They defend these against other males and mate with females entering their territory. Females lay their large (around ¹⁄₂₀₀ in or 1.5mm long) eggs in soft rotted bark or wood just above the water line of a tree hole. The eggs are unusual in that their hatching time varies from 4 to 184 days. This is thought to increase the chance that some will hatch when no predators are present in the hole. The carnivorous aquatic nymphs feed on insects and tadpoles living in the water of the tree hole. The nymphs are cannibalistic and usually only one survives to maturity in every 2–4 pints (1–2 liters) of water. They take about four months to develop from egg to adult.

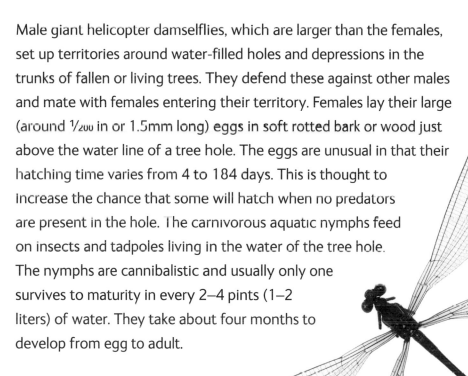

Giant Water Bug

WORLD'S HEAVIEST BUG

Maximum weight (adult, sex unknown):
¾ oz (25 g)

Scientific name: *Lethocerus maximus*

Distribution: Much of tropical South America

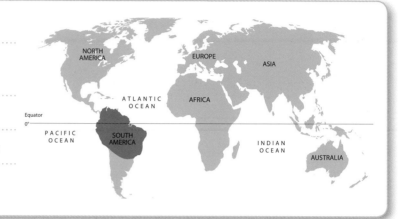

The giant water bug was only recognized as being different from the similar-looking *Lethocerus grandis* in 1938, even though specimens of it had been collected a long time before then. The giant water bug is the larger of the two and with a weight of ¾ oz (25 g) it is the largest aquatic insect in the world.

◀ Relying on their camouflage, giant water bugs stay motionless until their prey is in range and then grab it rapidly with their pincer-like front legs. They then stab their sharp, pointed mouthparts into the victim and inject saliva, which kills it and digests its body contents. The body juices of the prey are then sucked out. The bite of the giant water bug is very painful to humans.

▶ This record-sized female from Peru is in the collection of Bill Becks (UK), and has a wingspan of 8½ in (215 mm). The paddle-like middle and hindlegs are used for swimming, and the two structures at the end of the abdomen are used for breathing. They are pushed up through the water's surface and air is pulled down and then stored mainly under the wings. This image is life-size.

Giant water bugs live among aquatic vegetation in ponds and lakes and are voracious predators of aquatic insects, tadpoles and fish. Females lay a batch of around 150 eggs on a plant stem above the water's surface and this is guarded by the male, who also prevents the eggs from drying out. The eggs hatch after about eight days and the young are miniature versions of the adults, but lack wings. Males and females are similar in size and appearance. Adults fly at night and are attracted to artificial light, which is when they are most often seen.

Although this species has a very slightly smaller maximum wingspan than the empress cicada (see pp.28–29), it has a longer body and it is very likely the heavier of the two. The largest known specimens have wingspans of 8½ in (215 mm) and body lengths (excluding the wings) of 4¹/₁₆ in (103 mm).

Empress Cicada

BUG WITH GREATEST WINGSPAN

Maximum wingspan (adult male):
8½ in (217 mm)

Scientific name: *Megapomponia imperatoria*

Distribution: Southern Thailand, Peninsular Malaysia and Singapore

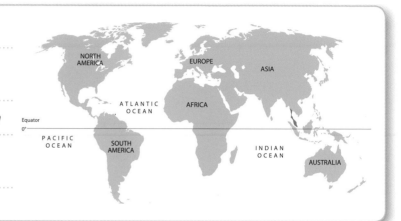

Female cicadas lay their eggs in slits that they cut in tree branches with their ovipositor, or egg-laying tube, and after hatching the young nymphs drop to the ground. Cicada nymphs look very different to the adults. They have mole-like forelegs and live in cells or burrows they dig underground. There they feed on the xylem sap of plant roots using their beak-like mouthparts. Xylem fluid is not very nutritious, as it is mostly water, and possibly because of this cicada nymphs often take several years to mature. When they are ready to transform into adults they construct an exit hole at the surface

▶ **This male empress cicada from Peninsular Malaysia, in the collection of Bill Becks (UK), has a wingspan of 8¼ in (210 mm) and a body length of 3 in (74 mm). It is shown life-size.**

of the soil capped by a hollow mud tube up to 9¾ in (250 mm) tall. They crawl up this tower at night, break through the top of it and then climb up a nearby tree trunk or plant stem. The exoskeleton of the nymph then splits and the winged adult emerges. Adult male and female empress cicadas look very similar and have similar wingspans.

Adult male cicadas sing to attract females. The empress cicada only calls for about 30 minutes at 7 p.m., high up in the forest canopy. The song is said to be extremely loud and is probably one of the loudest sounds produced by any insect. It is produced by stiff membranes called tymbals on the sides of the abdomen, which are vibrated by powerful muscles. Adults are found throughout the year, but are most abundant from March to May.

The largest known specimens are two males from the Cameron Highlands of Peninsular Malaysia in the collection of David Williams (U.S.). They both have wingspans of 8½ in (217 mm) and body lengths of 2¾ in (70 mm).

▲ Empress cicadas live in the rainforests of the Malay Peninsula and Singapore, with doubtful records from Borneo. They are found from sea level to about 4,921 ft (1,500 m) altitude and although fairly common, they are rarely seen except when attracted to artificial light at night.

▼ The transparent wings of the empress cicada, which are obvious here, make it difficult for predators to see it in its natural habitat.

Colossus Earwig

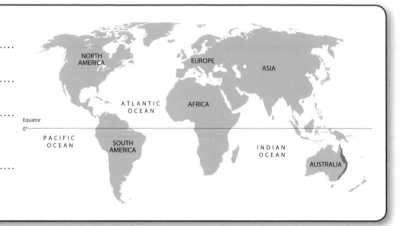

▼ A living specimen of a Colossus earwig. This species lacks wings and the males and females look very similar. It has been said that the formidable forceps can draw blood.

The Colossus earwig is found in the rainforests and wet *Eucalyptus* forests of eastern Australia, where it lives in or under rotting logs and among leaf litter. Despite its great size (for an earwig!) the Colossus earwig is secretive and not frequently seen. Unlike most insects, female earwigs carefully turn and clean their eggs to prevent them getting fungal diseases. When they hatch, the young earwigs look like miniature adults. Most earwigs are omnivorous and eat living and dead plant and animal matter, but a few of them are herbivorous and others are active predators. It is not known what the Colossus earwig feeds on.

Although the Colossus earwig is smaller in total length than the Saint Helena giant earwig, their body lengths are almost the same, and since the Colossus has a chunkier body it is very likely that it is the heavier of the two.

▶ The largest known specimen is this adult male, from Mount Tambourine, in Queensland, Australia, in the Natural History Museum, London. It has a total length of 2½ in (63 mm); its forceps are ¼ in (10 mm) long. This image is life-size.

Saint Helena Giant Earwig

WORLD'S LONGEST EARWIG

Maximum body length (adult male):

2$\frac{1}{8}$ in (54 mm)

Scientific name: *Labidura herculeana*

Distribution: Saint Helena Island in the South Atlantic

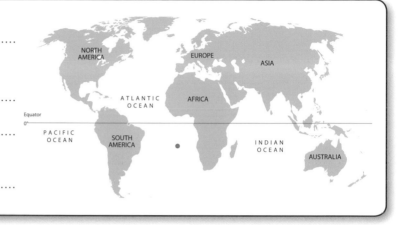

This immense earwig was only found on the remote island of Saint Helena in the South Atlantic. It was given its scientific name in 1798 by the Danish zoologist Fabricius and specimens seem to have only been collected three times since then: one in 1913, and 40 between 1965 and 1967 by two expeditions from the Royal Museum for Central Africa, Belgium. Since 1967, no living giant earwigs have been found, and sadly, it has probably become extinct, possibly due to habitat destruction and/or predation by accidentally introduced predators such as the huge centipede *Scolopendra morsitans*. Horse Point Plain, where this earwig was found, is dry and stony with small bushes and tufts of grass. The earwig was nocturnal and was found under stones, or near burrows in the soil. The Belgians reported that adult giant earwigs appeared during the summer rains and sought shelter underground at the onset of dry weather.

The longest known giant earwig specimen is a male in the Royal Museum for Central Africa, which has a body length of 2$\frac{1}{8}$ in (54 mm) and a total length of 3$\frac{1}{16}$ in (78 mm) including its forceps.

▼ The forceps of the male are much longer than those of the female and may be used in courtship or mating. Earwigs also use their forceps for feeding and defence.

◄ An adult male Saint Helena giant earwig with total body length of 2$\frac{1}{4}$ in (57 mm), now in the Natural History Museum, London. Although this species has small forewings, the hindwings are absent and the species is flightless. It is shown life-size.

Rhinoceros Cockroach

WORLD'S HEAVIEST COCKROACH

Maximum weight (adult female):
1¹⁄₈ oz (33.45 g)

Scientific name: *Macropanesthia rhinoceros*

Distribution: Eastern Queensland, Australia

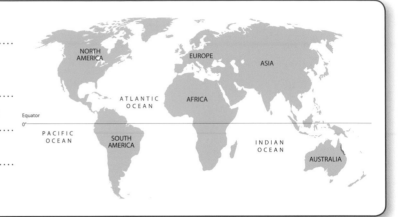

▲ **This massive wingless cockroach is found in a variety of habitats, ranging from dry** *Eucalyptus* **woodland, to** *Acacia* **scrub and, occasionally, rainforest.**

All of the habitats this cockroach is found in have one thing in common – compacted sandy soils. The soil texture is important because this species lives in permanent burrows, which it digs using its spade-like forelegs. These burrows commonly meander just below the soil surface for up to 3¼ ft (1 m) before sloping steeply downwards. They are usually about 15¾ in (400 mm) deep and as they descend they widen, before narrowing again near their end.

Rhinoceros cockroaches are nocturnal, only leaving their burrows to forage for food or, in the case of adult males, to search for mates. Unusual for cockroaches, they feed on dry plant debris such as dead leaves and the bark of twigs, which they drag down into their burrow and pack into the tunnel to feast upon at leisure. During the dry season of May to November they remain in their burrow feeding on the litter they have stored there.

▲ Males have a scoop-like pronotum (the large plate above the head) which is used for fighting and turning over rival males. Adult male rhinoceros cockroaches can measure up to 3¼ in (85 mm) in length and females are slightly smaller. This image is life-size.

Rhinoceros cockroaches are usually solitary but adult males sometimes live with females that are almost mature. Females of this species give birth to fully developed nymphs rather than laying eggs. About twenty nymphs are produced and they stay in the mother's burrow for about five months, feeding on the litter she has accumulated there, before leaving to dig their own homes. Nymphs take three to four years to mature, and in captivity adults can live up to seven years. Adults and large nymphs can hiss by expelling air from their last pair of abdominal spiracles (tiny breathing holes in the exoskeleton). They hiss when disturbed, when courting and fighting. Fighting is commonest between adult males. Each male lowers his pronotum, the plate above his head, and then they butt each other. The loser often gets turned over.

The heaviest known individual of this species was a female, probably pregnant, which weighed 1⅛ oz (33.45 g). This is about 558 times heavier than the common pest German cockroach (*Blattella germanica*)! Usually adult rhinoceros cockroaches weigh around ½ oz (19 g).

▶ The forelegs look like the front legs of a mole and are used for digging burrows in the sandy soils where the cockroach lives.

Gargantuan Cockroach

COCKROACH WITH GREATEST WINGSPAN

Maximum wingspan (adult female):
7¼ in (185 mm)

Scientific name: *Megaloblatta blaberoides*

Distribution: From Belize, through Central America into western Ecuador

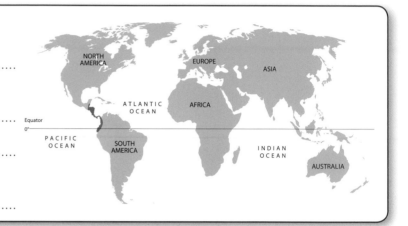

This huge species lives in rainforest from northern South America up into Central America as far north as Belize. What gargantuan cockroaches eat in the wild is unknown, but in captivity they have been successfully fed on a rather unusual diet of honey and boiled rotten wood.

▶ An adult female gargantuan cockroach with wings spread. Males and females of this species look very similar, but females are slightly larger. This image is life-size.

▲ Like most cockroaches this species is nocturnal and during the day it hides under loose bark, on dead tree trunks and under piles of decaying leaves.

▲ The eggs are enclosed in a hard ootheca or egg case, which the mother hides so that predators can't find it. This measures around 1½ in (40 mm) long and contains about 40 eggs, which take several months to hatch. This image is life-size.

The nymphs of this species are black, with an orange head and legs, and an orange spot on each side of the upper surface of the first five abdominal segments. This conspicuous coloration probably serves as a warning to potential predators that the nymphs can defend themselves. When threatened they produce a loud rasping noise by rubbing together special structures between two of the segments on the underside of their abdomen. Nymphs of this species have a layer of gray sticky slime on the upper surface of their last two abdominal segments. If a nymph is attacked by an ant or another predator, it moves its body around so that the hind part of the abdomen is directed towards the attacker. If the slime comes into contact with the attacker it rapidly turns into a rubbery glue, which can gum up and totally immobilize small predators.

The largest known specimen of the gargantuan cockroach is a female from Andagoya, in Colombia, South America, collected in 1957. This is in the collection of the Smithsonian National Museum of Natural History in Washington. It has a wingspan of 7¼ in (185 mm), its body length is 2½ in (66 mm) and its total length including the folded wings is 4 in (100 mm).

War-like Termite

WORLD'S BIGGEST TERMITE

Maximum weight (queen): 1¾ oz (50 g)

Scientific name: *Macrotermes bellicosus*

Distribution: West, Central and East Africa, from the Republic of Guinea to Tanzania

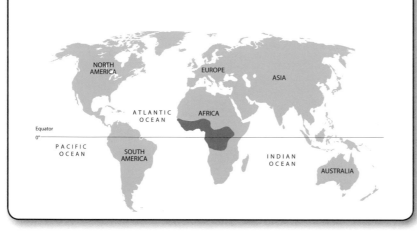

All the individuals in a war-like termite colony are the offspring of a single queen and king, which live in a clay chamber called the queen cell located deep in the center of the nest. Queens have massively swollen abdomens full of eggs that they lay constantly 24 hours a day. The queen of a closely related species was found to produce about 30,000 eggs per day, or 10 million per year. The royal pair and their colony are thought to survive for up to 20 years. Established colonies have the following castes, each of which plays a different role: major and minor soldiers with huge heads and jaws, which defend the nest; major and minor workers, which do all the work in the nest; and winged male and female reproductives, which fly out of the nest early in the rainy season and start new colonies. The soldiers and workers are sterile, eyeless and wingless.

▲ The war-like termite lives in open habitats in huge colonies of several million individuals. Its nest is a big earthen mound with a large cavity filled with fungus comb. A shaft runs up the center of the mound and another runs down through the center of the fungus comb. The architecture of the nest keeps the temperature at a fairly constant 86°F (30°C) and the humidity at around 90%. The tallest mound ever recorded was from the Congo and was 42 ft (12.8 m) high.

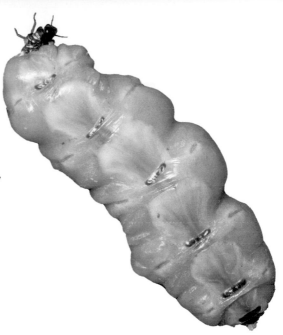

Older war-like termite workers bring back pieces of leaf litter and dead wood to the nest through underground galleries. Young workers then chew it up and swallow it, but they cannot digest it and it passes rapidly through their gut. They use their droppings containing the broken-up plant material to build the spongy fungus comb, which takes up most of the interior of the nest. A special fungus named *Termitomyces* grows in the comb, breaking down the plant matter and converting it into fungal tissue. The fungus produces nutrient-rich nodules and it is these that are the sole food source of the termites. The soldiers, the royal pair and the reproductives are fed by the young workers.

The heaviest reliably weighed war-like termite queen was collected in the Côte d'Ivoire in West Africa. She had an abdomen measuring 4¾ in (120 mm) and weighed 1¾ oz (50 g). It is likely that queens can get even heavier, as they are known to reach a length of up to 5½ in (140 mm) and a diameter of 1¼ in (35 mm).

▲ Mature queens have massively distended abdomens and are egg-producing machines. They are fed by workers that remove the eggs as they are laid (an egg is being laid in the image). The queen weighs up to 538 times more than when it was young and had wings. This living queen is shown life-size.

▼ Worker termites bringing back plant debris to the nest. The younger workers then chew and swallow it, and the droppings are used to make up the fungus comb, which takes up most of the inside of the nest.

▼ Termites are actually social cockroaches and, like cockroaches, they have nymphs that grow larger through a series of moults. The young termites live on the fungus comb near the queen cell.

Giant Asian Mantis

WORLD'S HEAVIEST PRAYING MANTIS

Maximum weight (adult female): ¼ oz (9 g)

Scientific name: *Hierodula membranacea*

Distribution: Nepal, India, Sri Lanka and Myanmar

▲ **The giant Asian mantis is a rainforest species, which lives in India and surrounding countries. It possibly also occurs in Thailand, Cambodia and China, but records of it in Java are doubtful.**

This mantis ranges from green to brown in color, which helps to conceal it in the bushes and trees where it lives. Like all mantids, this species is carnivorous. Small nymphs feed on small insects, while the adults tackle much larger prey, sometimes even small vertebrates such as tree frogs, lizards or mice. Mantids have large eyes and flexible neck muscles allowing them to turn their heads a full 180°, so they can follow prey while their body remains motionless. When the prey is close they grab it with their powerful spiny forelegs, which can strike out at incredible speed.

Males of the giant Asian mantis approach potential mates very cautiously. The male freezes when the female looks at him and he walks towards her only when she looks away. They have good reason

◀ Females of this species have a body length of up to about 3½ in (90 mm) and the males up to about 3⅛ in (80 mm). A well-fed female was found to weigh ¼ oz (9 g), making it the heaviest reliably weighed mantid known. The female mantid is illustrated life-size.

▲ The giant Asian mantis has well-developed wings and both sexes can fly. Females become too heavy to fly once they start producing eggs.

to be careful because females frequently attack and eat males, often just after they have finished mating. Mantids lay their batches of eggs in a frothy liquid that hardens and protects them until the nymphs hatch. They can produce several of these egg cases, or oothecae, during their lives and each contains around 150 eggs. The eggs hatch in about six to eight weeks. When the young mantids emerge from the ootheca they are covered in a membrane that is shed after a few minutes. Males take about 105 days to become adult from hatching and females take about 130 days.

Giant Stick Mantis

WORLD'S LONGEST PRAYING MANTIS

Maximum body length (adult female):
6¾ in (172 mm)

Scientific name: *Ischnomantis gigas*

Distribution: Senegal, southern Mauritania, Burkina Faso, Mali, northern Nigeria, northern Cameroon and Sudan

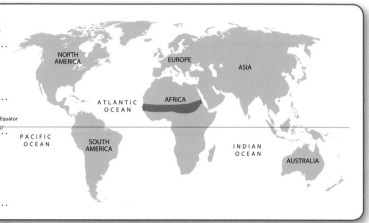

◀ This mantis lives in the Sahel region of Africa, some 2,400 miles (3,862 km) below the Sahara desert, from the Atlantic Ocean in the west, to the Red Sea in the east. The vegetation is open woodland with grass, scattered bushes and thorny acacia trees.

Although this species was described and named in 1870, little is known about its biology and ecology and there are few specimens in museum collections.

The giant stick mantis is known to live on bushes, where its brown coloration makes it look just like a twig. Adult females have very small wings and can't fly, whereas males have much longer wings and are known to fly. Males probably need to fly so that they can find females, and females probably use their short wings as part of their threat display – raising them and their forelegs in an aggressive manner towards potential predators.

 The record-sized female with a body length of 6¾ in (172 mm) in the collection of the Natural History Museum, London. It was collected in Kankiya, northern Nigeria. It is shown here life-size.

▲ **Male giant stick mantids are smaller than females and can reach 6¼ in (158 mm) in length with a similar wingspan. This male has a body length of 6⅛ in (156 mm). It is shown here life-size.**

Chan's Megastick

WORLD'S LONGEST INSECT

Maximum body length (adult female):
14 in (357 mm)

Scientific name: *Phobaeticus chani*

Distribution: Sabah (Borneo Island), Malaysia

NORTH AMERICA
EUROPE
ASIA
ATLANTIC OCEAN
AFRICA
Equator
0°
PACIFIC OCEAN
SOUTH AMERICA
INDIAN OCEAN
AUSTRALIA

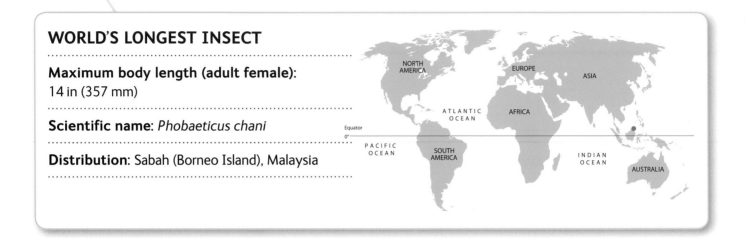

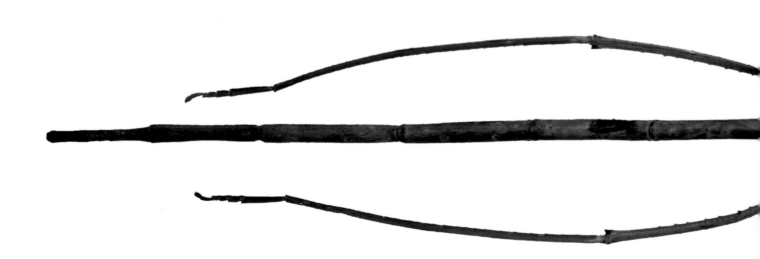

▲ **This is the record-breaking female, collected in February 1989 at Ulu Moyog in Sabah's Penampang district now in the collection of the Natural History Museum, London. The hole in the abdomen is where eggs were removed for study. It has a body length of 14 in (357 mm). Its total length would be ¼ in (6 mm) or so greater but the ends of its forelegs are missing. It is shown here life-size.**

Chan's megastick is the longest of all the world's insects and the extraordinary thing is that it was only given its scientific name in 2008. The first specimen to be found, a male, was collected 25 years before this, but it was only after the much longer female of the species was collected in 1989 that Dr. Phil Bragg, an expert on the stick insects of Borneo, realized that the species was new and decided to name it.

Chan's Megastick
continued

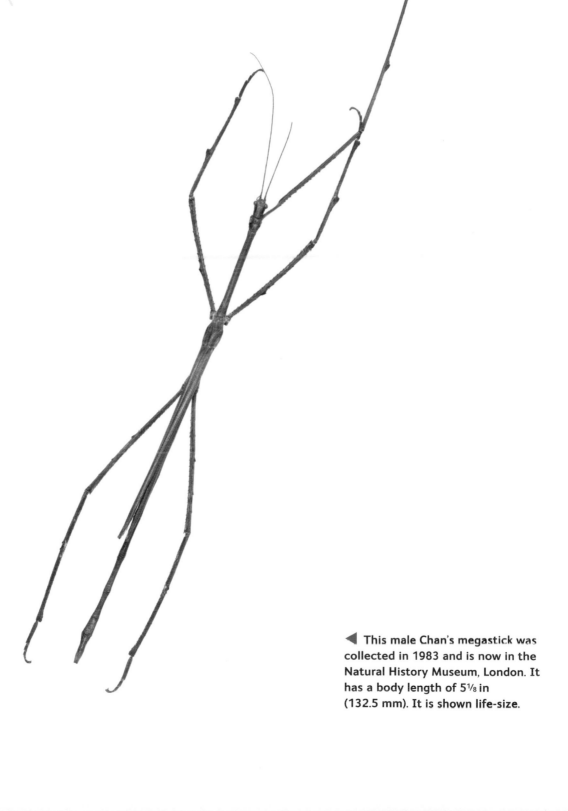

◄ This male Chan's megastick was collected in 1983 and is now in the Natural History Museum, London. It has a body length of 5⅛ in (132.5 mm). It is shown life-size.

Males and females of Chan's megastick are rather different. The female is wingless, much larger, dark green with whitish blotches, and with large spines on its middle and hind-legs. The smaller male has wings, is mostly brown, perhaps with greenish patches, and lacks large spines on its legs. Living females probably mimic lichen-covered twigs, while the males probably mimic smaller brown twigs. Stick insects remain motionless during the day, only becoming active after dark. All are herbivorous, but whether Chan's megastick feeds on the leaves of many plant species or only a few remains to be discovered.

As in closely related species, females of Chan's megastick probably lay one egg at a time, simply dropping it to land where it may. The eggs have a total length of ¼ in (9.4 mm) and their shape is probably unique in the insect world, with curved wing-like structures on either side of the egg capsule. The function of these "wings" is unknown, but they may either increase its resemblance to a particular winged plant seed, or perhaps they actually function like the wings of plant seeds,

catching the breeze as the egg falls from the forest canopy. This would carry the eggs away from the tree the mother is in, helping the offspring to disperse. Currently, nothing is known about the life-cycle of Chan's megastick, but in closely related species the eggs take 5–8 months to hatch, the nymphs take 6–8 months to become adults, and adults live for 6–8 months in the case of females, and as little as 3 months in the case of males.

▲ The rounded egg of Chan's megastick close up showing the curved wing-like structure on either side of the egg capsule.

The lowland rainforest in Sabah, Borneo is home to Chan's megastick. It probably lives high up in the forest canopy.

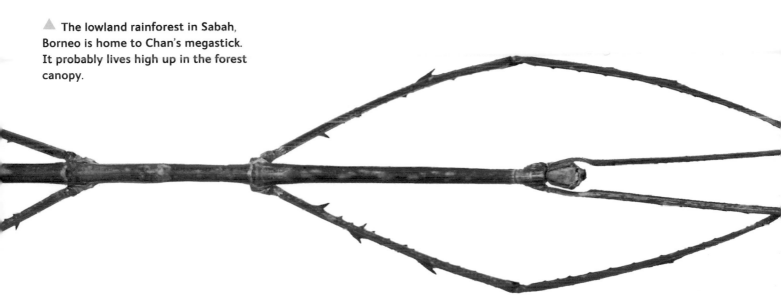

Currently only two females and four males of Chan's megastick are known. They were all collected in the Malaysian state of Sabah in northern Borneo between 1983 and 1994. They were found in rainforest in four separate localities ranging in altitude from about sea level to 5,249 ft (1,600 m). It is therefore likely that this species is fairly widespread in Sabah. The likely reason it eluded capture for so long is that it probably lives in the crowns of huge rainforest trees.

Giant Jungle Nymph

WORLD'S HEAVIEST STICK INSECT

Maximum weight (adult female):
1¾ oz (51.2 g)

Scientific name: *Heteropteryx dilatata*

Distribution: Thailand, Peninsular Malaysia, Singapore, Sarawak (Borneo), Sumatra and possibly Java

When this species was named in 1798, only one specimen (an adult female) was known to Western naturalists. A few years later in 1806, it was sold at auction for the equivalent of an astonishing $1,230 U.S. today!

This species lives in rainforest from around sea level up to about 5,249 ft (1,600 m) altitude. Like all stick insects, it is herbivorous and feeds on a variety of plants, mostly bushes, small trees or vines. Jungle nymphs are nocturnal and in some localities in Peninsular Malaysia they are very common. Females are usually green, but very rarely they are mustard yellow with green undersides. They can reach 6½ in (166 mm) in body length and are much bulkier than the males, which have a body length of up to 4 in (100 mm). Females have reduced wings and, unlike the males, they cannot fly.

The adult females curve their abdomen upwards when they are threatened, then extend and raise their hindlegs, and produce a hissing sound by rubbing their forewings and hindwings together. They try to grab the potential predator with their spiny hindlegs, and may also try to bite. Males also curve their abdomen up and raise their legs, but they cannot produce sound. If the threat persists they fall off the plant they are on and feign death, sometimes displaying their brightly colored hindwings.

Females lay eggs into soil in batches of about six using their long pointed ovipositor, or egg-laying tube. The eggs take between 8 and 18 months to hatch and the nymphs take 12 months (males) or 15 months (females) to reach adulthood. The adults can live for up to two years, at least in captivity.

The heaviest reliably weighed jungle nymph was an adult female with a body length of 5½ in (140 mm) kept at London Zoo in 1977. She weighed 1¾ oz (51.2 g).

▲ When at rest with the wings folded, the mottled brown coloration of the male gives it a resemblance to a twig. The pink hindwings are only visible when the males fly or when they open them as a threat display. This male is life-size.

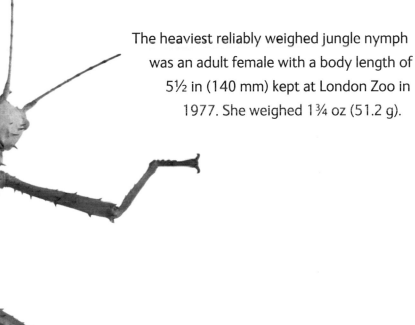

◀ Female jungle nymphs remain motionless amongst leaves during the day and are difficult to spot. Droppings of this species have been, and perhaps still are, used by local people in Malaysia to treat a number of ailments ranging from asthma to diarrhea. They are dissolved in hot water and drunk like tea. This specimen is life-size.

▲ Jungle nymph eggs measure about ¼ in (9 mm) in length and are one of the largest eggs of any insect.

Wetapunga

WORLD'S HEAVIEST ORTHOPTERAN

Maximum weight (adult female): 2½ oz (71.3 g)

Scientific name: *Deinacrida heteracantha*

Distribution: Little Barrier Island off the northeast coast of the North Island, New Zealand

"Wetapunga" is the name given to this spectacular weta by the Maori people, "Punga" being a Maori god who ruled over deformed and ugly creatures! The wetapunga is currently only found on Little Barrier Island, a 7,618 acre (3,083 h) forested nature reserve, which is now free of introduced cats and Pacific rats. Up until the mid-nineteenth century, the wetapunga was found throughout the northern part of the North Island, Waiheke Island and Great Barrier Island. The reason it became extinct in these areas is not known for certain, but the likely reason is predation by the introduced brown rat.

▼ When annoyed, wetapungas raise their spiny hind legs vertically and bring them forward above their head. They then kick backwards vigorously, making a rasping sound by rubbing structures on the leg and the abdomen together. They can also produce a hissing sound using structures between their abdominal segments. This is an adult male.

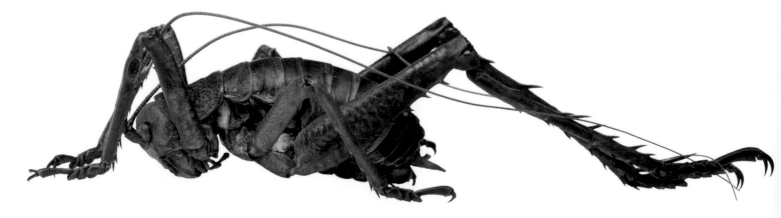

▶ **Adult wetapungas are completely wingless. They are surprisingly agile for their size, moving quickly if disturbed and capable of jumping quite large distances. Adult females are docile but males are aggressive. The sexes look similar apart from the female's ovipositor. This female is shown life-size.**

Wetapungas are nocturnal and usually live in trees, rarely coming down to the ground except to lay eggs. During the day they hide under loose bark, in tree holes and under dead leaves hanging down from tree ferns, palms and epiphytes. Wetapungas feed on the fresh foliage of a variety of plants, but can be cannibalistic in captivity.

Female wetapungas lay their oval brown eggs, which are about ¼ in (7 mm) long and ¹/₁₆ in (2.5 mm) wide, into soil using their ovipositor or egg-laying tube. The eggs are laid singly and a female might lay up to about 400 during her lifetime. The eggs take an average of 125 days to hatch and the nymphs pass through ten instars before becoming adults, a process which takes an average of 18.5 months. Adult females live an average of 141 days and males an average of 210 days. The entire life-cycle takes about 2.5 years.

Adult female wetapungas are about three or more times heavier than males. Females have a body length of up to 2¾ in (72 mm) and a total length of up to 4 in (103 mm) including the ovipositor. The average weight of captive mature female wetapungas at mating before laying eggs, was found to be 1¾ oz (49.7 g), with the heaviest female weighing a very impressive 2½ oz (71.3 g). This enormous individual mated several times and then laid ¾ oz (25 g) of eggs in nine days, which must have been a great relief! Not only is this female the heaviest orthopteran ever recorded, but it also gets the prize for being the heaviest adult insect known.

▼ **A huge living female wetapunga. Unlike their close relatives the grasshoppers, all bushcrickets have very long antennae.**

Imperial Bush-Cricket

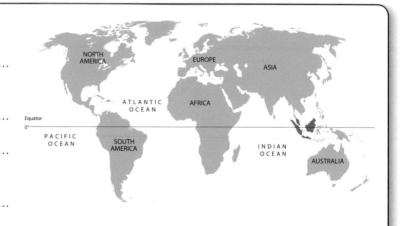

ORTHOPTERAN WITH GREATEST WINGSPAN: CONTENDER 1

Maximum wingspan (adult female):
10¾ in (274 mm)

Scientific name: *Arachnacris tenuipes*

Distribution: Peninsular Malaysia, Nias Island, Sumatra, Borneo, Java

The imperial bush-cricket is one of two contenders for the title of the orthopteran with the greatest wingspan – the other is the giant leaf bush-cricket (see p.50). Until recently, the imperial bush-cricket was usually known by the scientific name *Macrolyristes imperator* because it wasn't widely realized that *imperator* was actually the same species as *tenuipes*. The latter name was published in 1861, four years before the name *imperator*, so according to the rules laid down by the International Commission on Zoological Nomenclature the first name has to be used.

▲ The eggs produced by this species are very large – ½ in (16 mm) long and ¼ in (3 mm) wide. The female probably lays them into plant tissue using her blade-like ovipositor, where they are protected until they hatch.

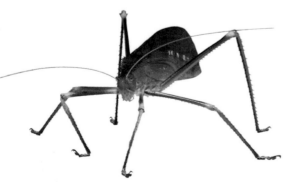

◄ Females lack the sound-producing structure on their wings that the males have. They have a blade-like ovipositor or egg-laying tube.

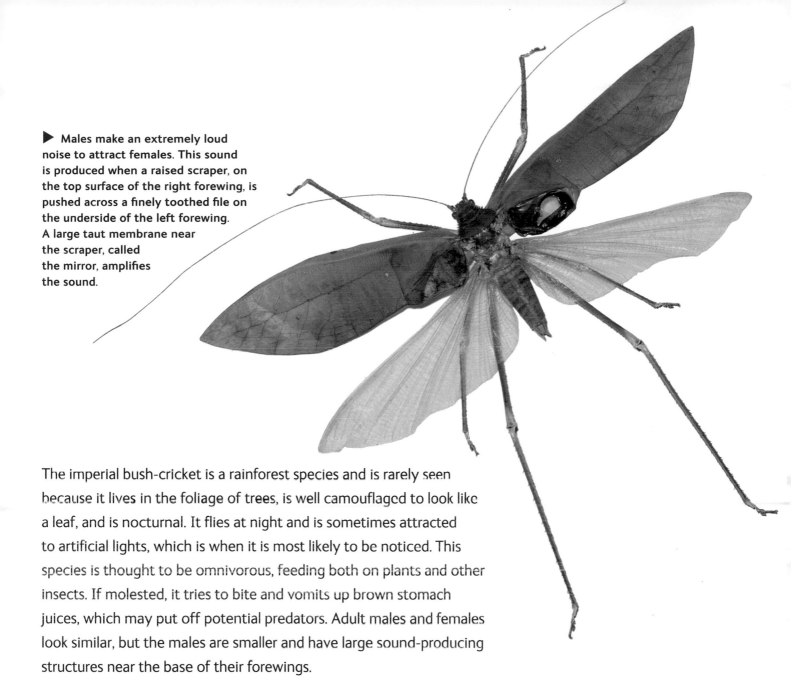

▶ Males make an extremely loud noise to attract females. This sound is produced when a raised scraper, on the top surface of the right forewing, is pushed across a finely toothed file on the underside of the left forewing. A large taut membrane near the scraper, called the mirror, amplifies the sound.

The imperial bush-cricket is a rainforest species and is rarely seen because it lives in the foliage of trees, is well camouflaged to look like a leaf, and is nocturnal. It flies at night and is sometimes attracted to artificial lights, which is when it is most likely to be noticed. This species is thought to be omnivorous, feeding both on plants and other insects. If molested, it tries to bite and vomits up brown stomach juices, which may put off potential predators. Adult males and females look similar, but the males are smaller and have large sound-producing structures near the base of their forewings.

The largest known specimens of the imperial bush-cricket are two females from Sabah, Borneo, which both have wingspans of 10¾ in (274 mm).

▼ A female specimen from Brunei, Borneo, with a length of 5¼ in (137 mm) from the head to the tip of its folded wings. It is shown life-size.

Giant Leaf Bush-Cricket

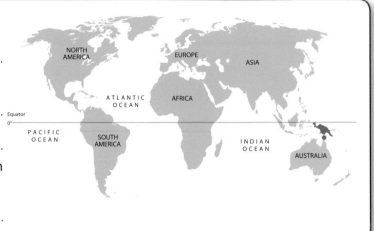

ORTHOPTERAN WITH GREATEST WINGSPAN: CONTENDER 2

Maximum wingspan (adult female):
10¾ in (271.6 mm), possibly 11 in (279 mm)

Scientific name: *Siliquofera grandis*

Distribution: Island of New Guinea, Goodenough Island, Aru Islands, and the northern Cape York Peninsula, Queensland, Australia

◀ The giant leaf bush-cricket is a rainforest species, found in the lowlands up to altitudes of about 3,937 ft (1,200 m). It lives in trees where it is very well camouflaged among the leaves.

This species is the second contender for the orthopteran with the greatest wingspan; the other is the imperial bush-cricket (see p.48). It is found on the huge island of New Guinea (where it seems to be relatively common), some surrounding islands, and also on the Cape York Peninsula in Australia (where it has only been collected a few times). Although this species is probably nocturnal and can fly, it is not attracted to artificial lights at night. They feed on leaves and are docile and slow moving. Females probably lay their eggs into plant tissue using their sharp ovipositor, or egg-laying tube.

This species belongs to a group of bush-crickets that lack sound producing structures on the male forewings. Instead, sound is produced by a series of parallel ridges near the base of the hindlegs. These rub against tiny pegs when the leg is moved in a certain way. Both sexes have these structures, but it is unknown whether both sexes produce sound and whether it is used to find a mate, courtship or some other purpose, such as scaring off potential predators.

There is a record of a female specimen of the giant leaf bush-cricket in the collection of the National Agricultural Research Institute (NARI) in Papua New Guinea with a wing "half-span" of over 5 in (127 mm). The distance between the wing bases is likely to be at least ¾ in (25 mm), so the wingspan would be around 11 in (279 mm). This would make it the champion of the orthopteran world for wingspan. Unfortunately, this specimen cannot be found so we cannot confirm this. Currently, the largest known specimen of this species is also one in the NARI collection. It is a female with a wingspan of 10¾ in (271.6 mm).

◀ An adult female giant leaf bush-cricket with its wings spread. Males and females look very similar, except the female is larger and has a conspicuous curved ovipositor. This image is life-size.

Fruhstorfer's Giant Dobsonfly

WORLD'S BIGGEST DOBSONFLY

Maximum wingspan (adult female): 8¼ in (214.5 mm)

Scientific name: *Acanthacorydalis fruhstorferi*

Distribution: Eastern China and northern Vietnam

▲ Fruhstorfer's giant dobsonfly lives in habitats like this mountain stream in the southeastern part of China.

This enormous species was discovered in 1907 and named after the famous German entomologist Hans Fruhstorfer. It is only known from the southeastern part of China and northern Vietnam, where it lives in mountainous areas at altitudes between about 820–5,413 ft (250–1,650 m). Adults fly from April to August and are always found near running water. They are attracted to artificial lights at night and there is a suggestion that they are also active during the day and drink the oozing sap of injured trees.

The larvae of Fruhstorfer's giant dobsonfly are aquatic, like those of all dobsonflies, and live in clean mountain streams, probably under rocks. They are carnivorous and probably feed on other aquatic insects. Dobsonfly larvae take a few years to mature and when they are ready to pupate they crawl out of the water and under a nearby rock or log. The pupae are unusual among insects in that they have functional jaws and can bite! After emerging from the pupa, adult dobsonflies generally only live a few days and don't eat solid food.

Females of this species are larger than the males and have powerful jaws, which can probably deliver a painful bite. The jaws of the males are hugely enlarged like those of a male stag beetle, and are probably used for fighting rival males and for holding the female during mating.

▲ A male from Guangxi Province, southern China, in the Natural History Museum collection. It has a body length of 4½ in (114 mm) and a wingspan of 7¾ in (196 mm). Its forewing length is 3½ in (92 mm) and the distance between the wing bases is ½ in (12 mm).

▲ The record-sized female from Guangxi Province, southern China in the Natural History Museum, London. It has a wingspan of 8¼ in (214.5 mm). Its forewing length is 4 in (101 mm) and the distance between the wing bases is ½ in (12.5 mm). It is shown here life-size.

Giant West African Antlion

WORLD'S BIGGEST NEUROPTERAN

Maximum wingspan (adult female):
7 in (177 mm)

Scientific name: *Lachlathetes gigas*

Distribution: Republic of Guinea and Sierra Leone in West Africa

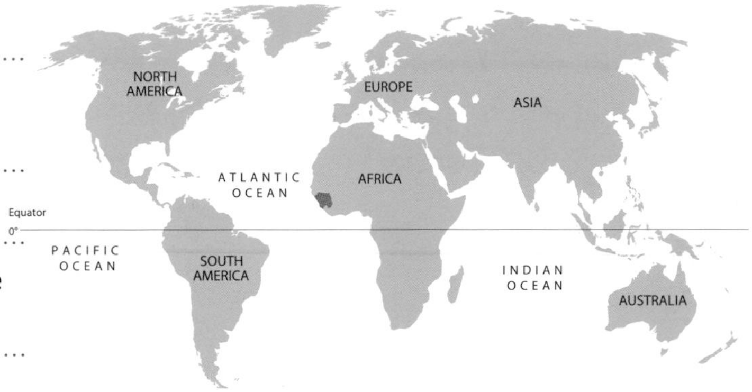

Virtually nothing is known about the giant West African antlion, even though it is the largest of all the world's 5,000 Neuroptera species and it has been known about since 1823 when it was named. Closely related species in southern Africa live exclusively in dry open habitats, so it is likely that this species lives in the savannah grasslands that cover parts of Sierra Leone and the Republic of Guinea. This is very probable as in 1957, four specimens were collected at the Ziéla station on Mount Nimba in the Republic of Guinea in an area that is largely grassland.

▼ A male giant West African antion, shown here life-size. The mottled wing pattern may camouflage the antlion among the vegetation.

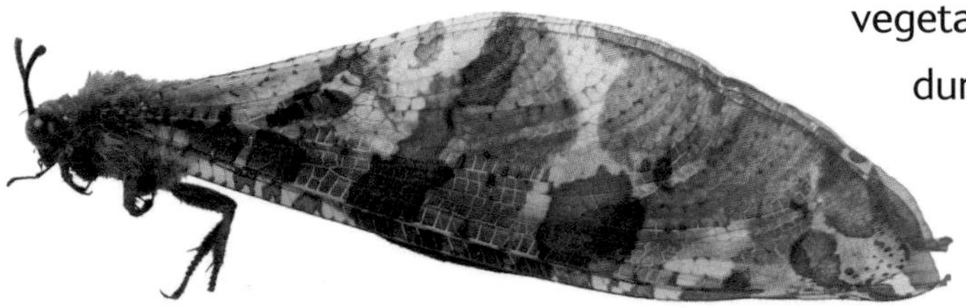

Adult males and females of this species look very similar, but females are slightly larger. They are probably nocturnal and rest on vegetation with their wings folded over their bodies during the day. Their mottled wing pattern probably camouflages them in the dappled light beneath vegetation. The adults and larvae of all antlions are carnivorous. The larvae of close relatives

live concealed just below the surface of loose sand or soil. They have plump bodies, large heads and long thin jaws and eat other creatures that come close enough for them to grab.

The largest known specimen of the giant antlion is a female with a wingspan of 7 in (177 mm) from Sierra Leone in the collection of the Natural History Museum, London.

▲ The giant West African antlion lives in savannah grassland like that shown here in Sierra Leone.

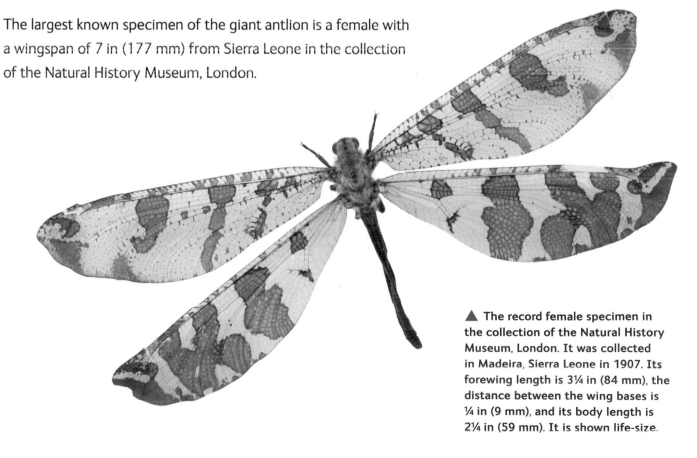

▲ The record female specimen in the collection of the Natural History Museum, London. It was collected in Madeira, Sierra Leone in 1907. Its forewing length is 3¼ in (84 mm), the distance between the wing bases is ¼ in (9 mm), and its body length is 2¼ in (59 mm). It is shown life-size.

Actaeon
Beetle

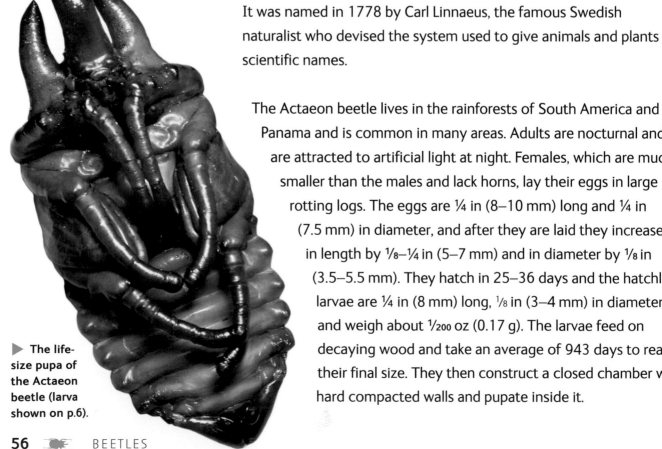

▶ The life-size pupa of the Actaeon beetle (larva shown on p.6).

Not only is the Actaeon beetle the heaviest of all the world's 350,000 beetle species, it is also the world's heaviest bug. It was named in 1778 by Carl Linnaeus, the famous Swedish naturalist who devised the system used to give animals and plants scientific names.

The Actaeon beetle lives in the rainforests of South America and Panama and is common in many areas. Adults are nocturnal and are attracted to artificial light at night. Females, which are much smaller than the males and lack horns, lay their eggs in large rotting logs. The eggs are ¼ in (8–10 mm) long and ¼ in (7.5 mm) in diameter, and after they are laid they increase in length by ⅛–¼ in (5–7 mm) and in diameter by ⅛ in (3.5–5.5 mm). They hatch in 25–36 days and the hatchling larvae are ¼ in (8 mm) long, ⅛ in (3–4 mm) in diameter, and weigh about ⅟₂₀₀ oz (0.17 g). The larvae feed on decaying wood and take an average of 943 days to reach their final size. They then construct a closed chamber with hard compacted walls and pupate inside it.

The pupal stage lasts about 38 days. In captivity, adult beetles live between 100 and 151 days, and feed greedily on fruit. Males can eat about 1¾ in (50 mm) of a banana per day!

The heaviest fully-grown larva of the Actaeon beetle recorded so far was a male bred in Japan in 2009, which weighed a staggering 8 oz (228 g). It became an adult beetle with a body length of 5⅛ in (130 mm). Its mother was collected in Satipo, Peru, and it took three years and three months for it to develop from hatching out of its egg to becoming an adult. The largest adult of this species ever recorded was a male with a body length of 5¼ in (135 mm), so its larva may have been even slightly heavier than the record-breaking larva from Japan!

Although adult males of the closely related Mars beetle, *Megasoma mars,* and the elephant beetle, *Megasoma elephas,* have similar maximum body lengths to the Actaeon beetle (5⅛ in or 132.7 mm and 5¼ in or 137 mm, respectively), the greatest reliably recorded weights of the larvae of these species are considerably lower (around 5½ oz, 160 g and 156 g, respectively). The reason for this is that the adult male Actaeon beetle has a larger, bulkier body and a relatively shorter head horn.

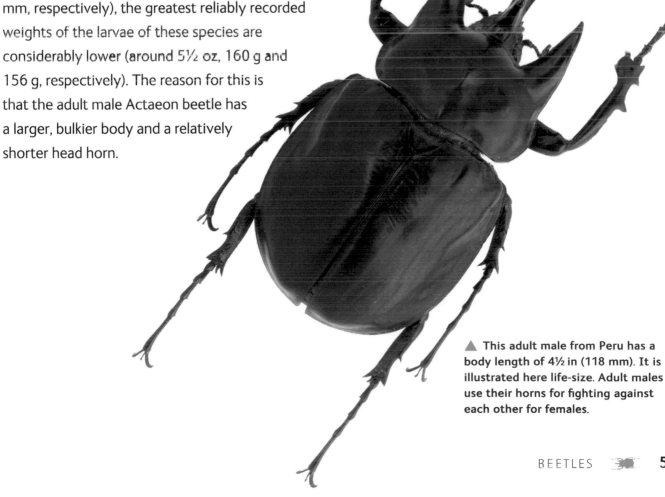

▲ An adult female Actaeon beetle with a body length of 2¾ in (70 mm). Females of the close relatives of this species all look fairly similar, unlike the males which all look very different.

▲ This adult male from Peru has a body length of 4½ in (118 mm). It is illustrated here life-size. Adult males use their horns for fighting against each other for females.

Hercules
Beetle

WORLD'S LONGEST HORNED BEETLE

Maximum body length (adult male): 6¾ in (172 mm)

Scientific name: *Dynastes hercules*

Distribution: Central America, Venezuela, Colombia, Ecuador, Peru, Bolivia, Brazil, Lesser Antilles, Trinidad and Tobago

▲ **Males use their horns to fight rival males. They make a soft squeaking sound when fighting or when alarmed, by rubbing the end of their abdomen against the inner surface of their wing cases. They are extremely powerful for their size – a male that weighed 1¹⁄₁₆ oz (30 g) was able to lift a weight of 4¼ lbs (2 kg) with its head horn!**

The Hercules beetle is the longest horned beetle in the world and the second longest species of beetle after the giant sawyer beetle. It lives in rainforest from sea level to 6,562 ft (2,000 m). This species is nocturnal and is often attracted to artificial lights.

Females lay their oval ⅛ x ⅛ in (3.5 x 4.3 mm) white eggs in the decaying trunks of a variety of species of hardwood trees. The eggs take about one month to hatch and the larvae feed on the soft rotting wood for 12–18 months (males), and 12 months (females). When fully grown, the larva makes an oval chamber with hard compacted walls and pupates inside it. The pupal stage lasts 2–2.5 months. Adults live for 3–12 months and feed on fruit and the oozing sap of damaged

▲ **A larva of the Hercules beetle. The heaviest larva so far recorded weighed 150 g (5¼ oz) and became an adult male with a body length of 165.2 mm (6½ in).**

trees, especially palms. Adults emerge after the start of the rainy season in June and they are most abundant between June and August.

The Hercules beetle has been divided up into about thirteen subspecies, which differ from each other in the size and shape of the male horns. The largest subspecies are *Dynastes hercules lichyi* from western South America and *Dynastes hercules hercules* from the islands of Guadeloupe and Dominica. The largest reliably measured individuals of this species are a 6¾ in (171 mm) male of the first subspecies, caught in Ecuador in March 2002, and a 6¾ in (172 mm) male of the second subspecies in a Japanese collection. A wild-caught male of *Dynastes hercules lichyi* measuring slightly over 6 in (150 mm) was found to weigh about 1¾ oz (50 g).

▲ A male Hercules beetle in flight. Like all beetles only the hind wings are used for flying. The forewings are wing covers.

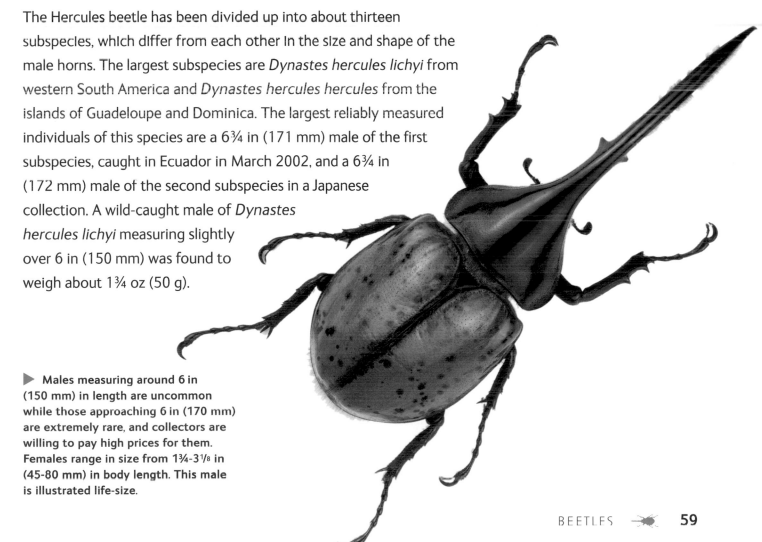

▶ Males measuring around 6 in (150 mm) in length are uncommon while those approaching 6 in (170 mm) are extremely rare, and collectors are willing to pay high prices for them. Females range in size from 1¾-3⅛ in (45-80 mm) in body length. This male is illustrated life-size.

Giant Sawyer Beetle

WORLD'S LONGEST BEETLE WITH ENLARGED JAWS

Maximum body length (adult male):
7 in (177 mm)

Scientific name: *Macrodontia cervicornis*

Distribution: Northern Venezuela and the Amazon Basin, and eastern Brazil

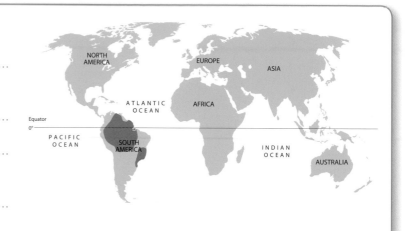

The male of the giant sawyer beetle is the world's longest beetle, but a significant proportion of its length is taken up by its greatly enlarged jaws. This species was named by Carl Linnaeus in 1758, based on a tiny female with a body length of 2½ in (63 mm), which is now in the Natural History Museum, London.

The giant sawyer is very widely distributed throughout the rainforests of South America east of the Andes, from the Atlantic rainforests of southeast Brazil to northern Venezuela. It is a fairly common species, frequently sold by dealers of dead insect specimens. However, since it is nocturnal and is not commonly attracted to light, this begs the question of how so many specimens can be available for sale. The likely reason is that local collectors know how to find the larvae, which they then rear to obtain the adults.

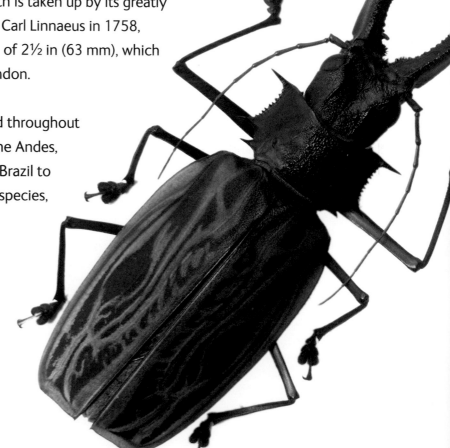

Female giant sawyers lay their eggs in dead or dying softwood trees, mainly palms, of a variety of species and the larvae create extensive galleries more than 3¼ ft (1 m) long and 4 in (10 cm) wide in the heart of the tree. The larvae look like long sausages and they can grow to 8¼ in (215 mm) long with an average diameter of 1¹/₁₆ in (28 mm). They are unusual for prionine beetles in that they are brown and covered with tiny hairs. Fully-grown larvae construct a chamber in the soil with compacted walls and pupate inside it. The pupal stage usually lasts between 15 and 21 days and the entire life-cycle is usually about two years long. A mature male larva 3½ in (92 mm) long was found to weigh 1½ oz (48 g) and produced an adult with a body length of 4¼ in (110 mm) and a weight of ½ oz (18 g), demonstrating just how much weight is lost during metamorphosis.

▲ **Female giant sawyer beetles are considerably smaller than males, with body lengths of between 2¼ and 4½ in (60 and 115 mm). Although the jaws of the female are much smaller than those of the male, they are more powerful.**

◄ **Male giant sawyer beetles range from 4 to 6¾ in (99 to over 170 mm) in length. This is the largest recorded specimen with a body length of 7 in (177 mm). It was collected in Peru in 2007 and was sold by insect dealer Michael Büche in 2009. It is shown life-size.**

Titan Longhorn Beetle

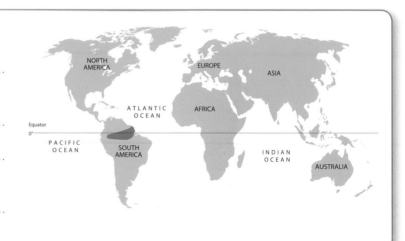

WORLD'S LONGEST BEETLE EXCLUDING HORNS AND JAWS

Maximum body length (adult male):
6½ in (167 mm)

Scientific name: *Titanus giganteus*

Distribution: Colombia, Ecuador, Peru, French Guiana and northern Brazil

This is the world's longest beetle, if jaws and horns are not taken into account. It was given the fitting species name *giganteus* in 1778 by Carl Linnaeus, who described it from a picture of a relatively small female illustrated in a book on Brazilian birds. For more than a century after its discovery, all of the very few specimens known were collected by local people who occasionally found them floating dead in a tributary of the Amazon, the Rio Negro, near the Brazilian town of Manaus. Because they were so rare, wealthy collectors were willing to pay very large sums of money to obtain one.

In about 1900, for example, a specimen fetched the princely sum of $240 U.S. at auction. This would be the equivalent of about $19,676 U.S. today!

▶ **This larva, which measures a whopping 7¾ in (200 mm) long and 1⅛ in (30 mm) in diameter, was collected from a rotting log in 1957 by Paul Zahl and is thought by many to be a Titan longhorn. Its weight is unknown. The larvae probably bore inside dead trees, possibly in the roots, and it is likely that they take several years to reach their maximum size. It is shown life-size.**

▶ **This male Titan longhorn beetle from French Guiana, has a body length of 5¼ in (139 mm). The adults often have mud on them, suggesting that they make their pupal cell in the soil. This specimen is shown life-size.**

A living individual of this species was finally observed in 1957 only 10 miles (16 km) downriver from Manaus, by zoologist Paul Zahl. Zahl's beetle had been attracted to the powerful floodlights of an oil refinery at night, and collectors have since realized that this species is rarely seen except when attracted to bright artificial lights, usually between 2:00 a.m. and 4:00 a.m.

Adult Titan longhorns emerge only during the height of the rainy season from mid-January to the beginning of March and live for 3–4 weeks. They do not feed – their sole objective is to find a mate. When threatened the adults produce a hissing noise and their powerful jaws can snap pencils in half and cut through human flesh! Females are very rarely seen, as unlike males, they are not attracted to light.

Female Titan longhorns are slightly smaller than males (4¾–6 in or 124–150 mm), but otherwise look similar. The largest reliably measured male was collected in January 1989 by Patrick Bleuzen in French Guiana, and was 6½ in (167 mm) long when dried. It was probably slightly longer when alive. Reports of specimens reaching up to and over 7¾ in (200 mm) are extremely doubtful and remain to be proven. A living 6 in (150 mm) male collected in French Guiana in 2005 weighed a not overly impressive 1⅛ oz (35 g).

▼ **A male Titan longhorn in flight. The average body length of males is about 5¼ in (135 mm) and specimens exceeding 6 in (150 mm) are rare.**

Giant Mydas Fly

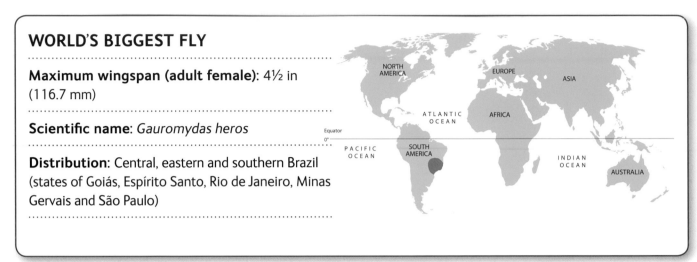
The giant mydas fly is fairly common in the dry forests of southern Brazil and also in the eastern Brazilian Atlantic forests above 2,296 ft (700 m). Males feed on flower nectar, whereas females apparently don't eat anything and live off the fat that they stored in their bodies when they were larvae.

▲ A male giant mydas fly, shown here life-size. Males are smaller and slimmer than females.

◀ Part of the fungus garden inside a leafcutter ant nest. The ants are large and small workers.

Male giant mydas flies defend territories around leafcutter ants' nests, and usually only one male is found around any one nest. These huge nests can be several meters across. If another male giant mydas fly approaches, an aerial battle ensues, leading to the defeat of one male. Males mate with females that venture into their territory. The female lays eggs inside the leafcutter ants' nest, and the larvae live among decaying plant debris in chambers in the nest where waste matter is stored. The larvae of several species of large beetle also live in these garbage chambers, feeding on the plant debris, and it is thought that the mydas fly larvae prey on them, sucking out their body juices.

▲ The ants take pieces of leaf back to their nest, chew them up and produce a compost, on which a special fungus grows. The ants then feed on the fungus. The old compost is thrown into garbage chambers, in which the larvae of the giant mydas fly live.

The largest reliably measured specimen of this fly is a female in the collection of the Museu de Zoologia, University of São Paulo, Brazil, which has a body length of 2¼ in (62.3 mm) and a wingspan of 4½ in (116.7 mm). Although no living specimens have been weighed this is the bulkiest and therefore probably the heaviest of all flies.

▲ When ready to pupate, the larva digs upwards out of the garbage chamber and makes a cell 4–7¾ in (100–200 cm) below the soil surface. When the pupa is ready to hatch, it pushes its way through the soil to the surface using strong spines. The adult fly hatches from it during the hottest time of day. The split at the top is where the adult fly emerged from.

◀ A giant female specimen of this species in the Natural History Museum, London, with a body length of 2¼ in (58 mm) and a wingspan of 4¼ in (112 mm). Shown here life-size.

Queen Alexandra's Birdwing Butterfly

WORLD'S BIGGEST BUTTERFLY

Maximum wingspan (adult female):
10¾ in (273 mm)

Scientific name: *Ornithoptera alexandrae*

Distribution: Southeastern Papua New Guinea
(Oro province)

Not only does the female of Queen Alexandra's birdwing have the greatest wingspan of all the world's 20,000 butterfly species, but this species probably has the heaviest caterpillar. The Queen Alexandra's birdwing butterfly was unknown to science until 1907, when Lord Walter Rothschild named it from a female sent to him from Papua New Guinea by the man who collected insects for him, Alfred Stanley Meek. Meek had blasted it out of the air with his shotgun using fine dust shot, a technique used by several early collectors of these huge insects, since they often fly very high and are difficult to catch with a net.

Queen Alexandra's birdwing is restricted to a small area of forest near the town of Popondetta in the Northern Province of Papua New Guinea. It is only known to occur in an area of 540 miles² (1,400 km²) and, because of its extremely restricted distribution, it is listed in Appendix I of the Convention on International Trade in Endangered Species (CITES), so all trade in specimens is strictly banned. Penalties for smuggling specimens can be severe.

▲ **The fully-grown caterpillar measures up to 4½ in (118 mm) long with a diameter of 1⅛ in (30 mm). The caterpillars are thought to store poisonous chemicals from their host-plant and their conspicuous coloration warns potential predators of this fact.**

◀ Large areas of forest, which were prime habitat for the butterfly, have regrettably been destroyed, firstly by the eruption of Mount Lamington in the early 1950s, but more recently by logging and clear-felling to make way for huge plantations of oil-palm trees.

Female Queen Alexandra's birdwings lay their light yellow ⅛ in (3.5 mm) diameter eggs singly on the undersides of the leaves of the plants they eat. A female might lay up to 240 during her lifetime. The caterpillars are only known to feed on two species of woody *Pararistolochia* vines, which can grow 131 ft (40 m) up into the upper canopy of the rainforest. The life-cycle from egg to adult takes more than four months, with adults living up to a further three months.

The females have an average wingspan of 8¼ in (210 mm), an average body length of 3 in (75 mm) and are reputed to weigh up to ¼ oz (12 g). The smaller males have wingspans of between 5¾–8¾ in (148–210 mm). It has been said that the wingspan of females can exceed 11 in (280 mm), but this needs to be confirmed.

▲ Male butterflies are usually more colorful than the females and this species is no exception.

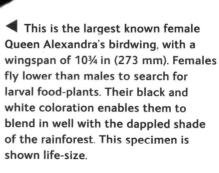

◀ This is the largest known female Queen Alexandra's birdwing, with a wingspan of 10¾ in (273 mm). Females fly lower than males to search for larval food-plants. Their black and white coloration enables them to blend in well with the dappled shade of the rainforest. This specimen is shown life-size.

Giant
Wood Moth

WORLD'S HEAVIEST MOTH

Maximum weight (fully grown larva): $1\frac{1}{16}$+ oz (31+ g)

Scientific name: *Endoxyla cinereus*

Distribution: Northern Queensland to southern New South Wales, Australia

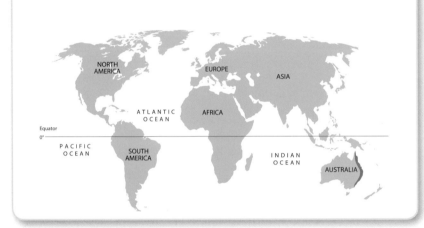

The giant wood moth lives in *Eucalyptus* woodland in eastern Australia, mostly towards the coast. Adults do not have functional mouthparts and live off the fat they stored as larvae. They only live a few days and during this time they mate. Females lay about 20,000 minute yellow eggs, covered in a protective sticky substance, into crevices in the bark of living *Eucalyptus* trees. After hatching, the $\frac{1}{32}$ in (1.5 mm) long caterpillars lower themselves down to the ground on silken threads and then disappear for about a year. They are thought to live underground and feed on roots during this time. When they reappear they are ¾ in (25 mm) long, as thick as a pencil, and have bold purple and white bands, probably as a warning to predators (older larvae are creamy with pale pinkish stripes).

▲ When the caterpillar is ready to pupate it makes an exit hole, which it seals with a curtain of silk mixed with sawdust. It moves to the end of its tunnel and seals itself off with a plug of sawdust. Then it pupates and when it is about to hatch it rotates and uses a sharp tooth on its head to cut around the plug like a can-opener. The plug falls down the burrow, the pupa wriggles down and pushes out the exit hole, and the adult moth then emerges to begin the cycle again.

Both sexes are a dull gray color, which serves to camouflage them when they are resting with their wings folded against their body on the bark of trees during the day.

This female in the Natural History Museum, London, is from Brisbane, Australia, and has a wingspan of 9¼ in (237 mm). It is shown life-size.

The caterpillars climb up the trunk of a smooth-barked *Eucalyptus* tree and bore a tunnel through the bark and into the sapwood. They feed on soft callus tissue the tree produces between the bark and the sapwood. The caterpillars live in the trunk for two years, enlarging the burrow and extending it upwards to a length of 7¾–11¾ in (20–30 cm). Female larvae grow to about 6 in (150 mm) long and 1⅛ in (30 mm) in diameter, while males are much smaller.

Female giant wood moths are the heaviest adult Lepidoptera, butterflies and moths, in the world and their wingspan is about double that of the males. The heaviest female ever recorded weighed 1¹⁄₁₆ oz (31.2 g), and the female with the greatest known wingspan measured 9¾ in (248.4 mm). It is very likely that this species has the heaviest caterpillar of any butterfly or moth, since caterpillars always weigh considerably more than the adults.

White Witch Moth

MOTH WITH GREATEST WINGSPAN

Maximum wingspan (adult female):
12⅛ in (308 mm)

Scientific name: *Thysania agrippina*

Distribution: Mexico to southern Brazil

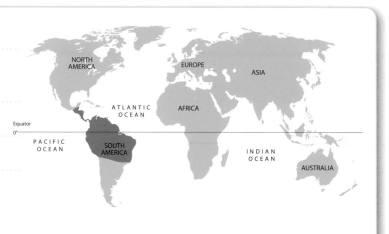

◀ The white witch moth is not uncommon and has an extremely large geographical distribution, ranging from the Rio Grande do Sul state in southern Brazil up through South and Central America to Mexico.

The white witch moth has the greatest wingspan of any living insect. It was given its scientific name in 1776 by the wealthy Dutch merchant and famous naturalist Pieter Cramer, who collected exotic butterflies and moths and named hundreds of new species. It is a rainforest species and, like most moths, it is nocturnal. The white witch moth remains motionless all day if it is not disturbed.

▲ During the day, it rests on the trunks of trees with its wings open, pressed against the bark to reduce its shadow. The white and black pattern on its wings camouflages it against the pale-colored lichens on the bark.

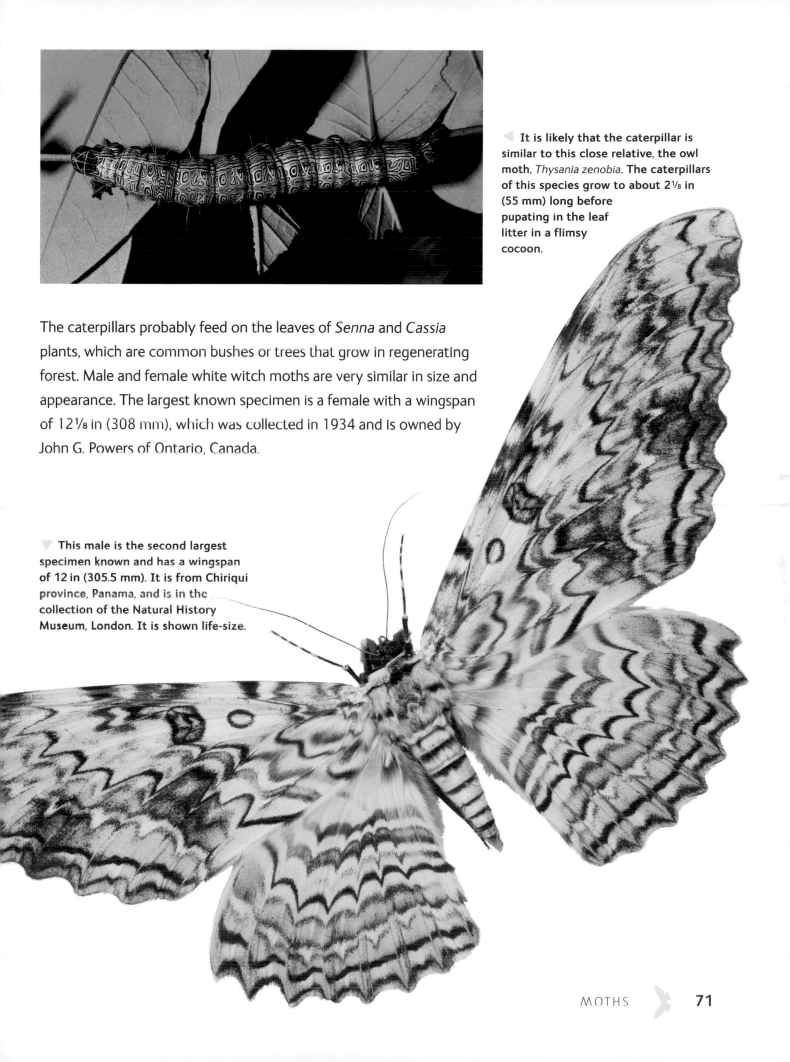

It is likely that the caterpillar is similar to this close relative, the owl moth, *Thysania zenobia*. The caterpillars of this species grow to about 2⅛ in (55 mm) long before pupating in the leaf litter in a flimsy cocoon.

The caterpillars probably feed on the leaves of *Senna* and *Cassia* plants, which are common bushes or trees that grow in regenerating forest. Male and female white witch moths are very similar in size and appearance. The largest known specimen is a female with a wingspan of 12⅛ in (308 mm), which was collected in 1934 and is owned by John G. Powers of Ontario, Canada.

This male is the second largest specimen known and has a wingspan of 12 in (305.5 mm). It is from Chiriqui province, Panama, and is in the collection of the Natural History Museum, London. It is shown life-size.

Hercules Moth

MOTH WITH THE GREATEST WING AREA

Maximum wing area (adult female): c. 44½ in² (288 cm²)

Scientific name: *Coscinocera hercules*

Distribution: Northern Queensland, Australia, island of New Guinea and surrounding smaller islands

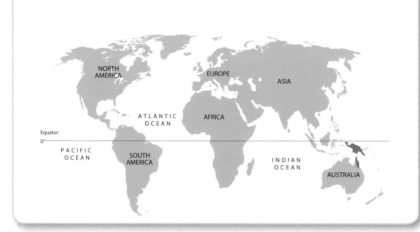

▲ Male Hercules moths are smaller than females. They use their feathery antennae to detect the scent (pheromones) produced by the females, thereby enabling the males to find the females and mate.

The Hercules moth is a fairly common rainforest insect though it is not often seen as it flies at night. The adults mainly fly from January to April, but a few also emerge at other times of the year. They do not have functional mouthparts and live only 5–8 days.

Females lay up to 230 rusty-red eggs, ¼ in (3 mm) in diameter, singly or in small batches, on a fairly wide range of rainforest trees. The eggs take 13–18 days to hatch. When ready to pupate, the caterpillars spin an elongate, double-walled silk cocoon inside a folded living leaf. The larva covers the stem of the leaf and the twig it is attached to with silk so that the leaf can't fall off, taking the cocoon with it. The cocoon is about 4 in (100 mm) long and 1⅛ in (30 mm)

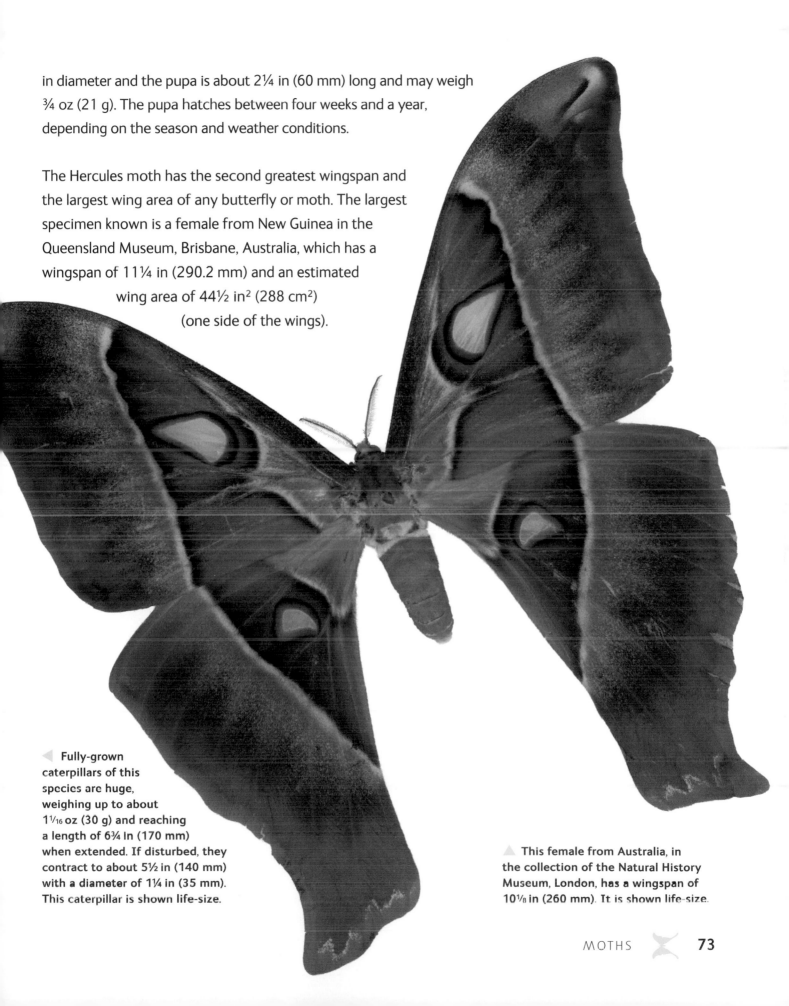

in diameter and the pupa is about 2¼ in (60 mm) long and may weigh ¾ oz (21 g). The pupa hatches between four weeks and a year, depending on the season and weather conditions.

The Hercules moth has the second greatest wingspan and the largest wing area of any butterfly or moth. The largest specimen known is a female from New Guinea in the Queensland Museum, Brisbane, Australia, which has a wingspan of 11¼ in (290.2 mm) and an estimated wing area of 44½ in² (288 cm²) (one side of the wings).

◀ **Fully-grown caterpillars of this species are huge, weighing up to about 1¹/₁₆ oz (30 g) and reaching a length of 6¾ in (170 mm) when extended. If disturbed, they contract to about 5½ in (140 mm) with a diameter of 1¼ in (35 mm). This caterpillar is shown life-size.**

▲ **This female from Australia, in the collection of the Natural History Museum, London, has a wingspan of 10⅛ in (260 mm). It is shown life-size.**

Giant Tarantula-Hawk Wasp

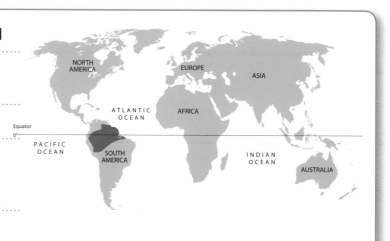

WORLD'S BIGGEST HYMENOPTERAN

Maximum wingspan (adult female): 4 ¾ in (121.5 mm)

Scientific name: *Pepsis heros*

Distribution: Guyana, Suriname, French Guiana and the Amazon Basin of Colombia, Venezuela, Ecuador, Peru and Brazil

This enormous wasp lives in the rainforests of northern South America and, although virtually nothing is known about its biology, it is likely to be similar to that of other tarantula-hawks. Adult tarantula-hawks feed on flower nectar and are active during the day. The sexes are similar in appearance but females are considerably larger than the males. Females search for tarantulas to feed their larvae on and, appropriately, the giant tarantula-hawk has been recorded as preying on the world's heaviest spider, the Goliath bird-eating spider, *Theraphosa blondi*, in Guyana (see pp.12–13). It must hunt one or more other tarantula species as well, since the Goliath bird-eating spider only occurs in the eastern part of the wasp's distribution.

▼ **A male giant tatantula-hawk wasp. Its body length is 1¼ in (36 mm).**

◀ Like all wasps, females can sting and males can't (the sting evolved from the female egg-laying tube called the ovipositor). Males are therefore believed to be mimics of females. Females are also mimicked by many otherwise relatively harmless animals, including bush-crickets like this one, assassin bugs, day-flying moths and even possibly a species of hummingbird.

When a female tarantula-hawk finds a spider, it approaches with its wings raised and grasps one of the spider's legs with its jaws. The spider tries to attack the wasp but the wasp nearly always wins and stings the spider on its underside, paralyzing it. The wasp then drags the spider to a burrow, perhaps even the spider's own, and lays an egg on its motionless body. The burrow is then sealed with a plug of soil and the egg hatches. The wasp larva feeds on the tissues of the still living spider, avoiding its vital organs, such as its heart. Just before the larva is ready to pupate it finally kills the spider. The larva then spins a cocoon nearby, out of which an adult wasp hatches to begin the cycle again.

◀ This very large female specimen of the giant tarantula-hawk wasp has a wingspan of 4¾ in (121 mm) and a body length (excluding the sting) of around 2¼ in (62 mm). It is from Suriname. The ¼ in (10 mm) sting is shown below. This female is shown life-size.

The largest known specimen of this wasp is a female from Yanachaga-Chemillén National Park in Peru, in a collection of the Universidad Nacional Mayor de San Marcos, in Lima, Peru, which has a wingspan of 4¾ in (121.5 mm).

Further Information

Amazonian giant centipede (*Scolopendra gigantea*): pp.8-9
The information of the record-sized dry specimen of the Amazonian giant centipede which is 13¾ in (350 mm) long, in the Muséum National d'Histoire Naturelle, Paris, is from Jean-Jacques Geoffroy (pers. comm., 2006). The record of an individual measuring 9¼ in (240 mm) in length and weighing 1⅛ oz (33.35 g) is from Spencer, Tainton and Rossiter (1999).

Giant African millipede (*Archispirostreptus gigas*): pp.10-11
The longest known giant African millipede with a body length of 15⅛ in (387 mm) is owned by Jim Klinger of Texas, U.S. (see http://www.guinnessworldrecords.com/records/natural_world/creepy_crawlies/largest_millipede.aspx, last accessed 05/10/09).

Goliath bird-eating spider (*Theraphosa blondi*): pp.12-13
The record of the heaviest captive female Goliath bird-eater, which weighed 6⅛ oz (175 g), is from Glenday (2009). The individual belonged to Walter Baumgartner from Austria.

Giant huntsman spider (*Heteropoda maxima*): pp.14-15
The record-sized male with a legspan of 11¾ in (300 mm) is the holotype in the Muséum National d'Histoire Naturelle, Paris. The gravid female with a body length of about 1¾ in (50 mm) is also preserved there. The record of the male Goliath bird-eating spider from Venezuela with a legspan of 11 in (280 mm) is from Carwardine (1995). It is possible that this individual was misidentified and that it was in fact a pinkfoot Goliath (*Theraphosa apophysis*), which looks very similar.

Giant vinegaroon (*Mastigoproctus giganteus*): pp.16-17
The records of the female with a weight of ¼ oz (12.4 g), the male with a weight of ¼ oz (10.2 g), and the female with a body length of 3⅛ in (82 mm) are from Fred Punzo (pers. comm., 2009).

Giant solifugids (*Galeodes arabs, caspius and granti*): pp18-19
A maximum weight of 1¾ oz (56 g) and a legspan of 4½ in (120 mm) is given for *Galeodes* by Moffett (2004). However, I have seen legspan measurements of up to 6 in (150 mm) cited in the literature, which may well be reliable. A maximum body length of 2¾ in (70 mm) is given by Hruskova-Martisová, Pekár and Gromov (2008) for *Galeodes caspius*.

Emperor scorpion (*Pandinus imperator*): pp.20-21
The record of emperor scorpions weighing more than 2¹/₁₆ oz (60 g) is from Polis (1990). The records of a male from Sierra Leone caught in 1977 that measured 9 in (229 mm) (and weighed 1¾ oz or 50 g), and a male from Ghana caught in 1931 with a body length of 8¾ in (228 mm), are from Wood (1982). Wood (1982) also mentions a record of a specimen of *Heterometrus swammerdami* caught in West Bengal state, India, in the 1940s, which measured 9 in (292 mm). However, this individual must have been measured from the tip of its sting to the tip of its outstretched claws, since the record body length of this species is about 6½ in (168 mm) (Polis, 1990). Lorenzo Prendini (pers. comm., 2009) says that he has seen specimens of the South African scorpion *Hadogenes troglodytes* up to 9¾ in (250 mm) in length, but I could not find any published records of specimens of this species longer than 8¼ in (210 mm).

Giant hawker dragonfly (*Tetracanthagyna plagiata*): pp.22-23
Wood (1976) states that the largest specimen of this species is the female holotype in the Natural History Museum, London with a wingspan of 7½ in (194 mm) and a body length of 4¼ in (108 mm). This specimen is badly damaged: its wings are detached and its thorax fragmented. I found that it has a forewing length of 3⅛ in (81 mm), so if we assume that the distance between the wing bases was ¼ in (8 mm), then it would have "only" had a wingspan of 6¾ in (170 mm). (Note that the hindwing is 3¹/₁₆ in, or 79 mm, long.) Because of the damage, it has been measured differently by different people. For example, the measurement in Wood (1982) was 7 in (176 mm).

The largest specimen of this species I know is a female from Borneo in the Natural History Museum, London, with a wingspan of 6¾ in (172 mm) (forewing length of 3⅛ in (82 mm), distance between wing bases of ¼ in (8 mm) and hindwing length of 3¹/₁₆ in (79 mm). Unfortunately its abdomen is damaged and has been replaced by a paper one.

Giant helicopter damselfly (*Megaloprepus caerulatus*): pp.24-25
The record-sized male is in the collection of the Natural History Museum, London, and was caught in 1988 by Steve Brooks at Estación Pitilla, Guanacaste National Park, Costa Rica. Its forewing length is 3½ in (92 mm), its hindwing length is 3½ in (89 mm) and the distance between its wing bases is ⅛ in (6 mm).

Giant water bug (*Lethocerus maximus*): pp.26-27
I know of two record-sized specimens with exactly the same wingspan (8½ in, or 215 mm): a female from Peru in the collection

of Bill Becks (UK); and one in the collection of David Williams (U.S.) (David Williams pers. comm., 2009). The maximum weight of this species was given by Cullen (1969).

Colossus earwig (*Titanolabis colossea*): p.30
Brindle (1970) said that the largest specimen in the Natural History Museum, London, had a body length of $2^{1}/_{16}$ in (53 mm) and forceps length of $^{1}/_{2}$ in (12 mm), giving a total length of $2^{1}/_{2}$ in (65 mm). However, my measurements of what is almost certainly the same specimen give an overall length of $2^{1}/_{2}$ in (63 mm), with the forceps being only $^{1}/_{4}$ in (10 mm) long.

Saint Helena giant earwig (*Labidura herculeana*): p.31
Measurements of the largest known male are from Brindle (1970). He also mentioned that a pair of detached forceps have been found which measure $1^{1}/_{4}$ in (34 mm) in length. It is therefore possible that the insect they came from had a body length greater than $2^{1}/_{8}$ in (54 mm).

Rhinoceros cockroach (*Macropanesthia rhinoceros*): pp.32-33
The record weight for this species of $1^{1}/_{8}$ oz (33.45 g) was given by Rugg and Rose (1991) but they did not state the sex of the specimen or its body length. However, given that it is so much heavier than the average adult of this species, it must have been a pregnant female.

Gargantuan cockroach (*Megaloblatta blaberoides*): pp.34-35
The record of the largest known gargantuan cockroach (a female from Andagoya, in Colombia, South America, collected in 1957) is from Gurney (1959).

War-like termite (*Macrotermes bellicosus*): pp.36-37
The record of the queen war-like termite from Côte d'Ivoire that weighed $1^{3}/_{4}$ oz (50 g) and had an abdomen $4^{1}/_{2}$ in (120 mm) in length is from Bordereau (1982). The records of queens measuring up to $5^{1}/_{2}$ in (140 mm) in length and of the tallest termite mound from the Congo, with a height of 42 ft (12.8 m), are from Wood (1982).

Giant Asian mantis (*Hierodula membranacea*): pp.38-39
The record of the female that weighed $^{1}/_{2}$ oz (9 g) was a personal communication from Martin Stiewe (UK) in 2007. Very few living mantids have ever been weighed and I would not be surprised if well fed and/or pregnant females of *Macromantis hyalina*, *Rhombodera fratricida*, *Plistospilota guineensis* or *Idolomantis diabolica* are eventually found to be heavier than this specimen.

Chan's megastick (*Phobaeticus chani*): pp.42-43
The record sized female of Chan's megastick is $1^{1}/_{2}$ in (40 mm) longer than *Phobaeticus kirbyi* from Borneo, the previous longest known stick insect species in terms of body length. The longest known specimen of *kirbyi* is the female holotype in the Natural History Museum, London, which has a body length of $12^{1}/_{2}$ in (317 mm). The greatest overall length recorded for *kirbyi* is $21^{1}/_{2}$ in (546 mm) (measured from the end of its foreleg to the end of its hindleg) for a female with a body length of $11^{1}/_{8}$ in (283 mm) from Brunei in Borneo (Hennemann and Conle, 2008), whereas the record female of Chan's megastick has an overall length of $22^{1}/_{4}$ in (567 mm). Chan's megastick also beats (by $^{1}/_{2}$ in, or 12 mm) *Phobaeticus serratipes*, which was the previous longest stick insect in terms of overall length. The largest known specimen of *serratipes* was a female from Peninsular Malaysia, which measured $21^{3}/_{4}$ in (555 mm) from the tip of its foreleg to the tip of its hindleg. Its body length was "only" 11 in (278 mm) (Seow-Choen, 1994).

In terms of overall length, Chan's megastick might have a short-lived reign as champion, because the female of the gargantuan stick insect (*Ctenomorpha gargantua*), a recently named species from north Queensland, Australia, might be even longer! Currently the female is only known from photographs of two living individuals, one of which has been calculated to measure an astonishing $24^{1}/_{8}$ in (615 mm) from the tip of its forelegs to the end of its greatly enlarged cerci (a pair of structures at the end of the abdomen, which are very short in most stick insects, but are greatly enlarged in this species) (Paul Brock, pers. comm., 2009) *C. gargantua* probably "only" measures $9^{3}/_{4}$ in (520 mm) from the tip of its forelegs to the end of its abdomen and its body length is probably "only" about $11^{3}/_{4}$ in (300 mm).

Giant jungle nymph (*Heteropteryx dilatata*): pp.44-45
The record for the heaviest known female of this species (2 oz, or 51.2 g) originates from Wood (1982).

Wetapunga (*Deinacrida heteracantha*): pp.46-47
The longest reliably measured adult female wetapunga (a dead pinned specimen) had a body length of $2^{3}/_{4}$ in (72 mm) and a total body length, including its ovipositor, of $4^{2}/_{32}$ in (103 mm) (George Gibbs, pers. comm., 2009). The heaviest known wetapunga, with a weight of $2^{1}/_{2}$ oz (71.3 g), was a female reared in captivity in New Zealand (Richards, 1973).

Imperial bush-cricket (*Arachnacris tenuipes*): pp48-49

The two record-sized females of this species with wingspans of 10¾ in (274 mm) are in the following collections: the Forest Research Centre of the Sabah Forestry Department (Chung, 2002); and the Academy of Natural Sciences in Philadelphia, U.S. (Hebard, 1922). At the time of writing the latter specimen could not be found.

Giant leaf bush-cricket (*Siliquofera grandis*): pp.50-51

Wood (1976) said that the "half-span" of a female of the giant leaf bush-cricket in the collection of the Papua New Guinea Department of Agriculture, Stock and Fisheries (National Agricultural Research Institute, NARI) was over 5 in (127 mm). Unfortunately, these specimens cannot now be found in the NARI collection (Sharon Agovaua and Charles Dewhurst, pers. comm., 2006).The largest specimen presently in the NARI collection is a female without collecting data, which has a wingspan of 10¾ in (271.6 mm). Its forewing length is 4¾ in (120.5 mm) and the distance between the wing bases is 1⅛ in (30.6 mm) (Sharon Agovaua and Charles Dewhurst pers. comm., 2006).

Actaeon beetle (*Megasoma actaeon*): pp.56-57

Information about the heaviest male Actaeon larva (8 oz, or 228 g) which was reared by Takayuki Suzuki in Japan, was taken from http://blogs.yahoo.co.jp/tasu9_or2/folder/476590.html (last accessed 05/10/09). The records of the largest adult males of this species (body length 5¼ in, or 135 mm) and the elephant beetle (*Megasoma elephas*) (body length 5¼ in, or 137 mm) are from: http://www.entnemdept.ufl.edu/walker/ufbir/chapters/chapter_30.shtml (last accessed 05/10/09). The largest reliably measured adult male Mars beetle (*Megasoma mars*) (body length 5⅛ in, or 132.7 mm) was captive bred in Japan (see http://www.geocities.com/kaytheguru/home.html, last accessed 05/10/09).

The heaviest recorded male larva of the Mars beetle was reared by Masaru Hozumi of Japan and weighed 5½ oz (160 g) (Yasuhiko Kasahara, pers. comm., 2006), while the heaviest male elephant beetle larva known weighed 5½ oz (156 g) and became a 5⅛ in (130.9 mm) adult beetle (Fujita et al, 2006). There are unconfirmed reports of elephant beetle larvae reaching a weight of about 6 oz (170 g).

Hercules beetle (*Dynastes hercules*): pp.58-59

Information about the heaviest recorded Hercules beetle larva (5¼ oz, or 150 g) is from http://www.geocities.com/kaytheguru/home.html (last accessed 05/10/09). The record of the 6¾ in (171 mm) *Dynastes hercules lichyi* from Ecuador is from Yasuhiko Kasahara (pers. comm., 2006) and the record of the 6¾ in (172 mm) *Dynastes hercules hercules* is from Mizunuma (1999). The record of an adult male *Dynastes hercules lichyi* weighing about 1¾ oz (50 g) is from Unno (2000).

Giant sawyer beetle (*Macrodontia cervicornis*): pp.60-61

The size of the mature larva (8¼ in, or 210 mm) is from Hogue (1993). Michael Büche (pers. comm., 2007) informed me that he had a male with a body length of 6¾ in (174 mm) and had heard of others this size. He has only ever had one male with a greater body length i.e. the record breaking 7 in (177 mm) specimen. Kazuhiko Iijima has seen a male with a length of 6¾ in (175 mm) in a Japanese collection (Yasuhiko Kasahara, pers. comm., 2006).

Titan longhorn beetle (*Titanus giganteus*): pp.62-63

The record for the largest reliably measured male Titan longhorn beetle from French Guiana (6½ in, or 167 mm) is from Bleuzen (1994). George McGavin (pers. comm., 2006) reported that a 6 in (150 mm) male he collected in French Guiana in 2005 weighed 1⅛ oz (35 g).

Giant mydas fly (*Gauromydas heros*): pp.64-65

The largest known specimen is a female in the Museu de Zoologia, University of São Paulo, Brazil, which was collected on 7th March 1937 in the Municipality of Itatiaia, Rio de Janeiro State, Brazil. It has a body length of 2¼ in (62.3 mm), a forewing length of 2¹/₃₂ in (52.3 mm), and the distance between its wing bases is ½ in (12.1 mm) (Carlos José Einicker Lamas, pers. comm., 2009).

Queen Alexandra's birdwing butterfly (*Ornithoptera alexandrae*): pp.66-67

The record-sized female specimen with a wingspan of 10¾ in (273 mm) in the Natural History Museum, London, was collected by A. S. Meek at the Kumusi River in 1907 for Walter Rothschild. It has a forewing length of 5⅛ in (132 mm) and the distance between its wing bases is ¼ in (9 mm). Its body length is 3 in (74 mm). The record of an adult female weighing up to ¼ oz (12 g) seems plausible and originates from Wood (1982). However, experts I have consulted think that this may have been a guess rather than a reliable measurement. The weight of ¾ oz (25 g) given for females by Carwardine (2007) is definitely an error, unless, perhaps, it had several shotgun pellets embedded in it!

Giant wood moth (*Endoxyla cinereus*): pp.68-69
The heaviest known adult female (which weighed 1¹/₁₆ oz, or 31.2 g) was collected in Byfield, Queensland in December 1994 and was weighed by Geoff Monteith (pers. comm., 2009). The female with the largest known wingspan (9¾ in, or 248.4 mm) is a specimen in the Queensland Museum (Geoff Monteith, pers. comm., 2009) . It has a left forewing length of 4¼ in (112.2 mm), a right forewing length of 4½ in (115.2 mm) and the distance between its wing bases is ¾ in (21 mm). Wood (1982) stated that there was a female with a wingspan of 9¾ in (250 mm) in the Natural History Museum, London, but the largest female I could find had a wingspan of 9½ in (242 mm) (forewing length 4¼ in, or 113.5 mm; distance between wing bases ½ in, or 15 mm; body length, 4 in or 102 mm).

White witch moth (*Thysania agrippina*): pp.70-71
The record-breaking female with a wingspan of 12¹/₈ in (308 mm) was collected in 1934 and is owned by John G. Powers of Ontario, Canada (Carwardine, 2007). The second largest specimen known (a male) was collected in Chiriqui province, Panama, and is in the collection of the Natural History Museum, London. It has a wingspan of 12 in (305.5 mm) (forewing length of 5½ in, or 144 mm; distance between wing bases of ½ in, or 17.5 mm; body length of 2½ in, or 63 mm).

Hercules moth (*Coscinocera hercules*): pp.72-73
Jack Hasenpusch informed me (pers. comm., 2009) that the heaviest Hercules moth caterpillar he has reared weighed just over 1²/₃₂ oz (30 g). Geoff Monteith told me (pers. comm., 2009) that the record-breaking female in the Queensland Museum with a wingspan of 290.2 mm (11¼ in) was donated to the museum by the famous 'Butterfly man of Kuranda', Frederick Parkhurst Dodd. Dodd said it was the largest specimen he ever obtained. It has a left forewing length of 5¼ in (138.5 mm), a right forewing length of 5¼ in (135.5 mm) and the distance between its wing bases is ½ in (16.2 mm). Geoff also informed me that the record in Wood (1982) of a female from Innisfail, Queensland, which reputedly had a wingspan of 14 in (355 mm), is an error. The Queensland Museum has this very specimen and it is not unusually large. An error was made when the size of it was reported by a local newspaper. The record in Wood (1982) of a female Hercules moth with a wing area of 100 in² (645 cm²) must be incorrect, since the specimen in question had a wingspan of 11 in (280 mm), which is ¼ in (7.5 mm) smaller than the record-breaking specimen, whose estimated wing area is 44½ in² (288 cm²).

Giant tarantula-hawk wasp (*Pepsis heros*): pp.74-75
The female specimen with the record wingspan of 4¾ in (121.5 mm) has a forewing length of 2²/₈ in (57 mm) and the distance between its wing bases is ¼ in (7.5 mm) (this probably would have been considerably greater if the thorax were not slightly crushed) (Gerardo Lamas, pers. comm., 2006). Its body length was measured at about 2¹/₃₂ in (52 mm), but its abdomen is very curved so this is an under estimation.

Wingspan or forewing length is probably a more reliable indicator of the overall size of *Pepsis* wasps than body length, since the length of the abdomen depends on how much the segments are extended. Lucas (1895) stated that the forewing of *Pepsis hyperion* can reach 58 mm (2¼ in), which, if correct, could mean that this is the largest *Pepsis* species. However, Lucas' specimens may have been misidentified or not accurately measured. Vardy (2000) in his extensive study of the genus *Pepsis*, found that of the 32,071 specimens of all known species he examined (including many of the specimens Lucas himself examined) – the species with the greatest body length was *Pepsis heros*, with a maximum body length of 2¼ in (63 mm). Unfortunately Vardy (2000) did not give wing lengths or wingspans for any of the specimens he studied.

References

Bleuzen, 1994. Prioninae 1: Macrodontini and Prionini. *Les Coléoptères du Monde*. Science Nat., France, Vol. 21. 92 pp.

Bordereau, C. 1982. Ultrastructure and formation of the physogastric termite queen cuticle. *Tissue and Cell*, **14**(2): 371–396.

Brindle, A. 1970. Dermaptera. La faune terrestre de l'ile de Sainte-Helene. *Annales du Musée Royal de l'Afrique Centrale, Tervuren, Belgique. Series 8, Sciences Zoologiques*, **181**: 213–227.

Carwardine, M. 1995. *The Guinness Book of Animal Records*. Guinness Publishing Ltd., 256 pp.

Carwardine, M. 2007. *Natural History Museum Animal Records*. Natural History Museum, London, 256 pp.

Chung, A. Y. C. 2002. Introducing the giant bush-cricket *Macrolyristes imperator*. *Malaysian Naturalist*, **56**(2): 48–51.

Cullen, M. J. 1969. The biology of giant water bugs (Hemiptera: Belostomatidae) in Trinidad. *Proceedings of the Royal Entomological Society of London, Series A*, **44**(7–9): 123–136.

Fujita, H. *et al.* 2006. Be-Kuwa Guinness. *Be-Kuwa*, Tokyo, **18**: 125–129.

Glenday, C. (Ed.). 2009. *Guinness World Records 2009*. Bantam Books, 608 pp.

Gurney, A. B. 1959. The largest cockroach. *Proceedings of the Entomological Society of Washington*, **61**(3): 133–134.

Hebard, M. 1922. Studies in Malayan, Melanesian and Australian Tettigoniidae (Orthoptera). *Proceedings of the Academy of Natural Sciences of Philadelphia*, **74**: 121–299.

Hennemann, F. H. and Conle, V. O. 2008. Revision of Oriental Phasmatodea: The tribe Pharnaciini Günther, 1953, including the description of the world's longest insect, and a survey of the family Phasmatidae Gray, 1835, with keys to the subfamilies and tribes (Phasmatodea: 'Anareolatae': Phasmatidae). *Zootaxa*, **1906**: 1–316.

Hogue, C. L. 1993. *Latin American Insects and Entomology*. University of California Press, Berkeley, 536 pp.

Hrušková-Martišová, M., Pekár, S. and Gromov, A. 2008. Biology of *Galeodes caspius subfuscus* (Solifugae, Galeodidae). *The Journal of Arachnology*, **35**: 546–550.

Lachaume, G. 1983. Goliathini 1: *Goliathus, Argyrophegges, Fornasinius, Hegemus. Les Coléoptères du Monde*. Science Nat., France, Vol. 3. 67 pp.

Lucas, R. 1895. Die Pompiliden-Gattung *Pepsis*. *Berliner Entomologische Zeitschrift*, **39**(4): 449–840.

Mizunuma, T. 1999. *Giant Beetles: Euchirinae, Dynastinae. Endless Collection Series Vol. 3*. Endless Science Information, Tokyo, 122 pp.

Moffett, M. W. 2004. Wind Scorpions. *National Geographic Magazine*, **206** (July 2004): 94–101. (Also see http://ngm.nationalgeographic.com/ngm/0407/feature5/index.html, last accessed 05/10/09)

Polis, G. A. 1990. *The Biology of Scorpions*. Stanford University Press, 587 pp.

Richards, A. M. 1973. A comparative study of the biology of the giant wetas *Deinacrida heteracantha* and *D. fallai* (Orthoptera: Henicidae) from New Zealand. *Journal of the Zoological Society of London*, **169**: 195–236.

Rugg, D. and Rose, H. A. (1991). Biology of *Macropanesthia rhinoceros* Saussure (Dictyoptera: Blaberidae). *Annals of the Entomological Society of America*, **84**(6): 575–582.

Seow-Choen, F. 1995. The longest insect in the world. *The Malayan Naturalist*, **48**(4): 12.

Spencer, W., Tainton, D. and Rossiter, S. 1999. The general husbandry, display techniques and breeding of the giant red centipede *Scolopendra gigantea* Linnaeus 1758 (Chilopoda: Scolopendromorpha) at Bristol Zoo Gardens. *Invertebrates in Captivity Conference 1999: Proceedings*. Sonoran Arthropod Studies Institute.

Unno, K. 2000. *Beetles*. Data House, Tokyo, 122 pp.

Vardy, C. R. 2000. The New World tarantula-hawk wasp genus *Pepsis* Fabricius (Hymenoptera: Pompilidae). Part 1. Introduction and the *rubra* species-group. *Zoologische Verhandelingen*, **332**: 1–86.

Wood, G. L. 1976. *The Guinness Book of Animal Facts and Feats*, second edn. Guinness Superlatives Ltd., 255 pp.

Wood, G. L. 1982. *The Guinness Book of Animal Facts and Feats*, third edn. Guinness Superlatives Ltd., 252 pp.

Index

Acknowledgments

I am deeply grateful to the many people who provided information or checked facts for this book. They are: Alan Stubbs (UK), Arthur Chung Yaw Chyang (Sabah, Malaysia), Atilano Contreras-Ramos (Mexico), Azman Sulaiman (Sabah, Malaysia), Bert Orr (Australia), Blanca Huertas (UK), Carlos José Einicker Lamas (Brazil), Chan Chew Lun (Sabah, Malaysia), Charles Dewhurst (Papua New Guinea), Christian Bordereau (France), Colin Vardy (UK), Dan Janzen (Costa Rica), Darren Mann (UK), David Jones (UK), David Rentz (Australia), Doug Yanega (U.S.), Edward Baker (UK), Fabian Haas (Kenya), Frantiek Kovaík (Czech Republic), Fred McDonald (Australia), Geoff Monteith (Australia), Geoff Thompson (Australia), George Else (UK), George Gibbs (New Zealand), George McGavin (UK), Gerardo Lamas (Peru), Greg Daniels (Australia), Harry Brailovsky (Mexico), Henrik Enghoff (Denmark), Jack Hasenpusch (Australia), Jamie Cranfield (UK), Jason Weintraub (U.S.), Jason Davis (UK), Jean-Jacques Geoffroy (France), John Cloudsley-Thompson (UK), John Lewis (UK), John Nielsen (Australia), Judith Marshall (UK), Leong Tzi Ming (Singapore), Ii-An-Shn (Taiwan), Lorenzo Prendini (U.S.), Malcolm Kerley (UK), Martin French (UK), Martin Honey (UK), Martin Stiewe (UK), Michael Büche (Spain), Michael Monaghan (Switzerland), Michel Sartori (Switzerland), Nelson Papavero (Brazil), Nigel Wyatt (UK), Oscar Conle (Germany), Paul Brock (UK), Paul Eggleton (UK), Per Christiansen (Denmark), Peter Jäger (Germany), Peter Weygoldt (Germany), Phil Bragg (UK), Randy Morgan (U.S.), Ray Gabriel (UK), Reinhard Ehrmann (Germany), Ricardo Palma (New Zealand), Richard Gallon (UK), Roger Roy (France), Rosser Garrison (U.S.), Rowland Shelley (U.S.), Sharon Shute (UK), Sharon Agovaua (Papua New Guinea), Steffen Bayer (Germany), Steve Brooks (UK), Steve Trewick (New Zealand), Stuart Hine (UK), Takayuki Suzuki (Japan), Ted Fenner (Australia), Warren Spencer (UK), Wilson Lourenço (France), and Xingyue Liu (China).

Very special thanks go to Bill Becks (UK) for allowing me to photograph specimens in his collection, to Yasuhiko Kasahara (a.k.a. Kay the Guru) (Japan) and David M. Williams (U.S.) for lots of valuable information, and to my wife Jan for giving me an enormous amount of help and support while I spent the weekends of summer 2009 writing this book. I am also extremely grateful to Jan for her help with writing the sections on arachnids and myriapods.

Picture Credits

Front and back cover including flaps:
Cicada © George Beccaloni. All other images © NHMPL.

All images © NHMPL, Natural History Museum Picture Library
unless listed below.
All maps Lisa Wilson © Natural History Museum.

p.1 top right © Dr Christian Bordereau; p.1 bottom left © George
Beccaloni; p.2 bottom Dorling Kindersley © Jerry Young ; p.3 bottom
© Auscape / ardea.com. p.4 Dorling Kindersley © Jerry Young; p.6
© Takayuki Suzuki; p.7 © Richard Bizley/Science Photo Library; p.8 top
© Pete Oxford / NPL; p.9 top © Stuart Hine; p.9 bottom © Jesús Molinari;
p.10 © Adam Jones/Science Photo Library; p.11 top © James Carmichael
Jr./NHPA; p.12 © John Mitchell/Science Photo Library; p.13 left © Barbara
Strnadova/Science Photo Library; p.13 right © George Beccaloni; p.14
© Nicholas Reuss/Lonely Planet Images; p.15 top © Tränkner /
Senckenberg; p.15 bottom © Ingo Fritzsche; p. 16 © Fred Punzo; p.17
top © Photo Researchers/NHPA; p. 17 bottom © Michael & Patricia
Fogden; p.18 © Sinclair Stammers; p.19 top © Wildlife/H.Kirk / Still
Pictures; p.19 middle © Daniel Heuclin/NHPA; p.19 bottom © Sinclair
Stammers; p.20 © Daniel Heuclin/NHPA; p.21 Jerry Young © Dorling
Kindersley; p.22 © Jan Beccaloni; p.23 top © Dr Leong Tzi Ming; p.24
top © Ola Fincke; p.24 bottom © John C Abbot; p.25 top © Michael &
Patricia Fogden; p.26 © Michael & Patricia Fogden/Minden Pictures/FLPA;
p.27 © George Beccaloni; p.28 © George Beccaloni; p.29 top © Michael
Durham/Minden Pictures/FLPA; p.29 bottom © Dr. Alexey Yakovlev; p.30

left © Steve Wilson; p.32 © Joel Iedema/Istockphoto; p.33 top
© Pavel German; p.34 bottom, p.35 top © George Beccaloni; p.35
bottom © OMNH; p.36, p.37 top © Dr Christian Bordereau; p.37 bottom
left © Prof. Renoux; p. 37 bottom right © Alexis Peppuy; p.38 © Ian
Lockwood/NPL; p.39 top © Rod Williams/NPL; p.39 bottom © Martin
Stiewe; p.40 © Dr David Haberlah; p.43 © Nick Garbut/NPL; p.44 Dorling
Kindersley © Jerry Young; p.47 top © George Gibbs; p.47 bottom © Mark
Moffett/Minden Pictures/FLPA; p.49 top, p.50 © George Beccaloni; p.52
© Dr Xingyue Liu; p.55 top © Alison D. Johnson; p.56 © Takayuki Suzuki;
p.57 bottom © George Beccaloni; p.58 top © Michael & Patricia Fogden;
p.58 bottom © Cameron Campbell; p.59 top © Kim Taylor/NPL; p.59
bottom © Pascal Goetgheluck/Science Photo Library; p.60 © Michael
Büche; p.61 © George Beccaloni; p.62 © Paul Zahl/National Geographic
Image Collection; p.63 top © George Beccaloni; p.64 bottom © Mark
Moffett/Minden Pictures/FLPA; p.65 top © George Beccaloni; p.65
middle © Carlos José Einicker Lamas; p.66, p.67 top © Biosphoto/BIOS/
Gilson Francois/Still Pictures; p.68 © Queensland Museum, Gary Cranitch;
p.69 top © Pavel German; p.70 left © Mitsuhiko Imamori/Minden
Pictures/FLPA; p.70 right © Arthur Grosset; p.71 top © Dan Janzen; p.72
bottom © Auscape/Ardea.com; p.75 top © George Beccaloni/Science
Photo Library; p.75 bottom © George Beccaloni.

Every effort has been made to contact and accurately credit all copyright
holders. If we have been unsuccessful, we apologize and welcome
correction for future editions and reprints.